Paul feared that he would find "quarrels, gossip, conceit, and disorder" in the  changed, especially in communities of Muslim background followers of Christ! Oksnevad and Adam's thoughtful work, *From Conflict to Hope: Voices from North African, Middle Eastern, and Iranian Christians,* tackles head-on the chronic conflict seen in these fledgling communities. Having lived for 35 years in the Middle East, I resonated with the difficulties exposed by the church leaders whose presentations form the backbone of the book. I wished it had been available decades ago. It overflows with insight into problems stemming from poor communication, distorted honor and shame, and toxic leadership. Pursuing qualities like accountability structures, transparency, willingness to ask forgiveness, and embracing weakness will help overcome these problems. This is a book that should be carefully read by anyone involved in church-planting among Muslim background people, particularly those from North Africa, the Middle East and Iran.

George Bristow, PhD; Senior Research Fellow,
Institute for the Study of Religion in the Middle East

From Conflict to Hope invites us into a 2022 consultation on leadership among believers from a Muslim background from Iran, the Middle East and North Africa together with intercultural workers in the region. Grace, hope and candour shape conversations about miscommunication, toxicity, conflict and shame. The contributors affirm that they are not alone but need the global church to both learn from and stand ready to help this emerging movement of followers of Jesus. This book's important lessons extend far beyond the geographic homelands of the contributors.

David Greenlee, PhD; missiologist, Operation Mobilisation

Tackling the most critical issues found within both Arab and Iranian cultural communities, this book is a crucial guide to understanding how to effectively minister within the Middle Eastern context. The numerous experts who contributed to the content of this book gives assurance to the reader that issues presented have been knowledgeably dealt with. A must read for those engaged in the praxis of ministry in the MENA region of the world.

Dr Marvin J Newell, Ambassador at Large, Missio Nexus, author of
A Third of Us: What it Takes to Reach the Unreached

This rare and excellent compilation of voices from the BMB community is crucial both for their flourishing and that of the broader Christian family. The contributors grapple with the overidentification of Christianity with Western culture (a problem for all Christians) while exploring various aspects of conflict and conflict resolution. Insightful discernment to be contemplated by believers of all backgrounds!

Todd M Johnson, Eva B. and Paul E. Toms Distinguished Professor of
Mission and Global Christianity at Gordon-Conwell Theological Seminary

The vast region covering North Africa, the Middle East and Iran is beset by diverse challenges and multiple conflicts. Christian churches of all kinds have to negotiate their way through difficult contexts which often involve not only discrimination but also active persecution. This is especially the case for churches consisting of Background Muslim Believers. Furthermore, conflict without can easily trigger conflict within. This present volume, carrying the voices of editors Oksnevad and Adam as well as a range of anonymous contributors from the region, serves as an invaluable signpost for all seeking to address conflict within BMB communities. The book skilfully mixes deep reflection with practical action. Diverse sub-themes relating to conflict are discussed: issues of communication, considerations of honor and shame, authority structures and the challenges of toxic leadership, methods of mediation, and many other concepts. The volume concludes with a presentation of practical steps that BMB churches in MENA and Iran, and beyond, can take to address the diverse challenges that they face. This book should not only provide guidance, but it should also give a sense of hope to BMBs in challenging contexts.

Professor Peter G Riddell, London School of Theology

For those praying that Muslims would turn to the Lord Jesus – thank God, your prayers are being answered! As might be expected, these new believers from Muslim background (BMBs) face an array of challenges as they serve in high-persecution contexts marked by intense spiritual warfare. *From Conflict to Hope* addresses one of these challenges – conflicts in the local church. This brief and readable book amplifies BMB voices as recorded in interviews and workshops. Readers will find *From Conflict to Hope* chocked full of practical advice and reflections in dealing with issues such as discipleship and communication, as well as toxic leadership and shame avoidance. Conflict mediators may provide a helpful role in restoring wholesome relationships in such settings. *From Conflict to Hope* comes to us in a timely manner.

Fred Farrokh, Director, Wasla Media Project

GLOBAL VOICES FROM A MUSLIM BACKGROUND

From Conflict to Hope

GLOBAL VOICES FROM A MUSLIM BACKGROUND

From Conflict to Hope
Voices from Emerging Indigenous Leaders of North African, Middle Eastern and Iranian Christians

Edited by

Roy Oksnevad and Sama Adam

Copyright © Roy Oksnevad and Sama Adam 2024

First published 2024 by Regnum Books International

Regnum is an imprint of the Oxford Centre for Mission Studies
St. Philip and St. James Church
Woodstock Road
Oxford, OX2 6HR, UK
www.regnumbooks.net

09 08 07 06 05 04 03 8 7 6 5 4 3 2 1

The rights of Roy Oksnevad and Sama Adam to be identified
as the editors of this work has been asserted by them
in accordance with the Copyright, Designs and Patents Act 1988.

All rights reserved. No part of this publication may be reproduced, stored in a retrieval system, or transmitted, in any form or by any means, electronic, mechanical, photocopying, recording or otherwise, without the prior permission of the publisher or a license permitting restricted copying. In the UK such licenses are issued by the Copyright Licensing Agency, 90 Tottenham Court Road, London W1P 9HE.

British Library Cataloguing in Publication Data
A catalogue record for this book is available from the British Library

ISBN (paperback): 978-1-917059-40-4
ISBN (eBook): 978-1-917059-41-1

Typeset by Words by Design
Printed and bound in Great Britain

Original cover concept by Amy and Kevin Schultz

GVMB Series Preface

Pat Brittenden, Jonathan Andrews and Paul Bendor-Samuel, series editors

We are delighted to bring this volume as an early contribution to the series of Global Voices from a Muslim Background being prepared by the **Hikma Research Partnership** and published by Regnum Books.

It addresses a topic critical to us, and we trust to all readers: how do these disciples experience leadership within fellowships of like-minded people.

We are inclined to think that many of the trickiest issues in ministry within Muslim-majority contexts lie in the ecclesiology rather than in the missiology. Why? There are many factors that shape fellowships and churches as they emerge, mature and interact with the global church. Expectations from both within the fellowship, the local context, the national context as well as fellow disciples of different ethnicities can vary widely. How can such fellowships be understood and supported as they seek to be authentic, faithful witnesses to Christ?

We believe that the two editors model the unity in diversity that we believe enriches the global church. One is female, the other male. Sama is from an Arab majority country and of Muslim heritage. Roy is from a Western country but knows Iran well. Their collaboration in the writing of this book has been a joy to behold, albeit not without its moments of tension. We commend them for how they have handled themselves as they strove to produce a book that truly reflects the breadth and depth of the material on which it is based.

We endorse Roy writing a chapter giving one way of exploring cultural dynamics and how these vary across diverse contexts. We trust that this gives Western readers in particular an insight into the background that those of Persian and Arabic majority cultures are raised within, and hence what they bring into fellowships as new believers and then as emerging leaders. Furthermore, this material also illustrates that Middle Eastern countries are culturally diverse.

It is our desire with this series to enable more such people to become active participants in Christ's mission, enriching the global church in the process.

Jonathan Andrews

We are enormously grateful to Dr Roy Oksnevad, and to Sama Adam for the painstaking, meticulous and expert way in which they have edited this volume. Anyone who has been involved in consultations and conferences will know how difficult it is to faithfully record the dynamic presentations and interactions that take place when brothers and sisters meet to talk about important issues. Reports of such gatherings have a purpose, but they only go so far. What you have in your hands is far more than a report. You have a snapshot of what was a remarkably engaging encounter of brothers and sisters – mostly of a Muslim background – from North Africa and the Middle East and the Persian Gulf. We use the word "snapshot" because, in many ways, this book is like a photo or short video of an event which happened at a particular time in place. Whilst the picture is a true reflection of what happened, it can never fully communicate the dynamics that were involved. And, of course, these conversations have all continued.

As series editors, we are delighted that the conversations addressing these thorny issues of communication, honour, and shame, conflict management and toxic leadership have begun.

Those of us actively involved in ministry among/with BMBs know them to be critical – even existential – matters facing the growth and maturing of BMB church communities.

Finally, we wish to point out that the two main editors of this volume, were mature experienced Christian leaders, teachers and practitioners, one BMB, one non-BMB. Sama and Roy's different backgrounds and perspectives enable them to approach the curating of all that which was shared at this consultation from their different vantage points. They represent the kind of robust, trusting and creative dynamic that occurs when brothers and sisters listen to each other, challenge each other and learn from each other, in so doing, Christ is glorified. We hope you appreciate the fruit of their labour as much as we have.

It is our desire with this series to enable more such people to become active participants in Christ's mission, enriching the global church in the process.

Pat Brittenden

Acknowledgements

I would like to thank Dr Roy Oksnevad who dedicated his time, his knowledge, and his skills to prepare for Towards The Goal consultation (TTG) and make sure that the consultation's recordings and material will be documented and well-presented in this book in order to benefit a wider audience. Dr Roy contributed great input to the book and without his hard work, this book wouldn't see the light.

Also, I want to thank all the TTG contributors and presenters – whose names remain anonymous in the book for various reasons – both for their contribution and for their work for the kingdom. We, the editors, know and value each of them.

Sama Adam

A book or a consultation is never the work of one individual. Therefore, I would like to thank the convening committee for their tireless work in putting together this extraordinary consultation. It provided a safe place where BMB and church leaders from North Africa, the Middle East, and the Iranian diaspora could address conflict and its sources in an open and honest manner. This consultation would not have happened without the expertise and connections brought by the convening committee.

I would like to single out key individuals who played a major role in bringing to fruition the TTG consultation and subsequent book. Stephen Kelley was instrumental in bringing together the members of the steering committee as well as logistics from ETC and Blackhawk Ministries. Mehrdad Fatahi and Don Little were invaluable for their wisdom and connections to the BMB community. The publication of this book is indebted to Pat Brittenden and the Hikma Project for their desire to bring the wisdom gleaned from this consultation to you the readers. Ricardo Zapata is the man behind all the technical and logistical help. He never complained even with all the changes thrown at him and the delay caused by COVID. I want to thank the eight presenters who videotaped the introductions to each topic which was so valuable in guiding the discussions that followed. I would like to thank Sama Adam for all her work and for the excellent discussions we had in preparing this volume. Lastly, I would like to thank my wife Darla whose keen eye for grammar and tuned ear to foreign accents unselfishly volunteered to transcribe the recorded sessions. She has been a true partner both in life and in ministry.

May Christ's church be richer and stronger through the cooperative spirit that was evident throughout this consultation and editing of this book. To God be the glory.

Roy Oksnevad

Contents

	GVMB Series Preface	vii
	Acknowledgements	ix
1	Introduction	1
2	Background Reflections on Discipleship: Conflict and Transformation	5
3	Communication: Can We Just Say What We Mean?	19
4	Honour and Shame: Living in the Shadows	31
5	Conflict from Toxic Leadership: "Someone Needs to Control the People"	41
6	Mediating Conflict Resolution: Can We All Just Get Along?	63
7	A Way Forward: Turning the Upside-Down Right Side Up	93
	Abbreviations	113
	Glossary	113
	References	115

1. Introduction

Mission organisations focused on the Muslim world write about the dramatic change in Muslims coming to Christ, which has been chronicled in the book, *A Wind in the House of Islam* (Garrison, 2014). Confronting the challenge of reaching a religion that is resistant to the gospel and even anti-Christian in its foundational sources has fostered multiple strategies and tools on how best to reach Muslims for Christ. Out of the urgency of the Lausanne conferences for world evangelisation have come multiple approaches for reaching the world for Christ and finishing the unfinished task of world evangelisation. Organisations like Joshua Project[1] are focused on identifying Unreached People Groups, while others are committed to methods that will launch a movement. Certain mission agencies are focused on launching discipleship-making movements with the role of missionaries being catalysts who will release a movement to Christ (Wilson, 2021). Their focus is on the task of evangelism and completing it. These agencies desire that these movements will be healthy and produce healthy disciples.

The task of world evangelisation is one aspect of the great commission. We are also to teach them to obey everything that Jesus commanded. New fellowships and churches that get planted also need to learn how to live in a sinful world. As churches grow, they will face conflict, not just from outside the church but also from inside the church.

We live in a fallen world in which conflict is part of the curse stemming from the Fall recorded in Genesis 3. Although conflict can have similar expressions in various cultures, there are cultural expressions that are uniquely shaped in each society. The focus of this book is to raise awareness of what a small segment of missionary academics and practitioners are observing, particularly in the North African, Middle Eastern, and Iranian contexts, where large numbers of people are coming to Christ (Garrison, 2014). They are raising concerns that believers from a Muslim background (BMBs) are facing challenges that need to be heard and not minimised (Durie, 2010, Little, 2015, Miller, 2016, Oksnevad, 2019).[2]

Conflict happens in every culture. People typically seek to *manage* conflict, whereas reconciliation or resolution of conflict, although rare, should be the

---

[1] Joshua Project, see website at: https://joshuaproject.net/.
[2] Significant books are Don Little, *Effective Discipling in Muslim Communities: Scripture, History and Seasoned Practices* (Downers Grove, IL: IVP, 2015); Duane Alexander Miller, *Living Among the Breakage: Contextual Theology-Making and Ex-Muslim Christians* (Eugene, OR: Pickwick, 2016); Roy Oksnevad, *The Burden of Baggage: First Generation Issues in Coming to Christ* (Littleton, CO: William Carey, 2019); Mark Durie, *Liberty to the Captives: Freedom from Islam and Dhimmitude through the Cross* (Melbourne, Australia: Deror, 2010).

norm in the Christian community. Interpersonal conflict, clashes over leadership and leadership styles, hypersensitivity over perceived offenses, and an inability to resolve conflicts are typical of a new church made up of new immature Christians. Since few bring a strong cultural understanding of resolving conflict, many yield to their cultural default response, such as denying the existence of conflict, trying to control it, or simply leaving the church when conflict arises.

In early 2019, Stephen Kelley, an Egyptian believer from a Muslim background (BMB),[3] brought together seasoned ministers working in the North African, Middle Eastern, and Iranian contexts to plan a consultation on discipleship, entitled *Toward The Goal* (TTG). Soon afterward, the world was engulfed in a pandemic, changing the way people could meet. In 2021, the decision was made by the planning committee to move ahead with the consultation virtually. To accomplish their objectives, they chose to deal with only one discipleship topic facing BMBs and their churches – conflict. Conflict is splitting churches; the inability to resolve conflict results in once-flourishing fellowships disbanding and former fellowship members not speaking to each other. The consultation brought together leaders from a Muslim background from three geographic regions which are Muslim majority, for the purpose of looking at conflict and sharing insights from an intercultural perspective, drawing on the wisdom that each community has learned and experienced.

It was recognised by the planning committee that cultural issues are often hidden when looked at through a monocultural lens. The perspective from those outside a particular cultural context can bring additional insight that one society is oblivious to. In addition, there are issues that are considered *haram* (forbidden) and often overlooked by the cultural protocols. The richness of this work is bringing together leaders from many countries, as well as outsiders who have lived or worked among Muslim background believers, to discuss the common concerns about conflict. The insights shared are deeper and richer through this intercultural exchange. It was discovered through this consultation that BMBs throughout the Middle Eastern, North African, and Iranian contexts have many challenges in common. But there is diversity expressed in certain ethnic groups. It was a surprise to the other two regions that the Iranian community had a richer understanding of the issues of discipleship than they previously thought. The desire of the conveners of this consultation is to see fellowships stabilised so they can bear much fruit. This is a battle for the soul of Christ's bride, the church.

The planning committee invited BMB church leaders from North Africa, the Middle East, and Iran to address conflict from their lived experiences rather than outsiders presenting lessons learned in other cultural contexts. In addition to looking into major cultural characteristics, the convenors (a combination of mature BMB and not BMB leaders) sought to give voice to BMBs through dialogue on what they are experiencing in their churches and fellowships. To do this, they divided the topic of conflict into four culturally appropriate areas: 1) conflict that comes from communication or the lack thereof; 2) conflict that

---

[3] Former Muslims identifying terms are not uniform. Muslim background believers (MBB) and just Christians are other terms used.

comes from chronic and cultural shame; 3) conflict that comes from toxic leadership; 4) conflict resolution through mediation. The main presenters for topics 1–3 were recognised BMB leaders in their countries. Conflict resolution through mediation was presented by Westerners who are considered outside-insiders, meaning that they are respected leaders in the indigenous church with excellent cultural and language skills. They are often called upon to mediate conflicts. This book will explore the unique cultural expressions of conflict and the role of mediators in addressing it.

Attendees

Ninety-six people registered for the event, fifty-eight participants (60%, the majority) were from the MENA region and Iran. Of these participants, seventy-one people participated at least in one session during the four days event.

Procedure for the 2022 Consultation

The following chapters contain parts of sections that were recorded. Each section had four distinct parts to allow for maximum opportunity to discuss what was presented. First, each topic was introduced with a pre-recorded 20-minute introduction presented by one Farsi-speaking and one Arabic-speaking leader. They are reproduced in each chapter. Second, the two presenters were joined by a moderator and another leader to discuss the topic in a live panel discussion. These panel discussions are not included here. Third, the attendees were placed in pre-selected breakout rooms to consider the relevance of the presentations to their ministry contexts. A moderator and a recorder were assigned to each group to guide the conversation forward. Fourth, the attendees returned to the large group where the recorders summarised the key points and action points discussed in their small groups. All the sessions were recorded via Zoom application and afterwards were collected to be written as scripts. In the process, we were keen to translate the Arabic and Farsi parts into English. The scripts were gathered and incorporated in the book. Some of the original presentations had to go through editing and rephrasing to be linguistically appropriate. Many presenters and other participants asked not to be identified in this book for various reasons.

This book records the presentations and the key elements of the various discussions. Many contributors do not want to be identified due to the sensitivity of their situations. Consequently, we have not named any of the participants. We have, however, endeavoured to ensure, at all points, that it is clear what is the context of the person contributing. Typically, we have distinguished by Iranian or Arab, in country or in diaspora, and for the case of Arabs whether they are in the Middle East or North Africa. A few contributors do use specific ministries in order to make their point.

The consultation was the place where we were seeking to provide the opportunity to hear from North Africans, Middle Easterners, and Iranians concerning their cultural context and how their people experience conflict. We encourage the reader to join us in the discussion and to seriously wrestle with what is happening in our Muslim background fellowships so we can hear the collective wisdom God has given to each one of us. We begin with a survey of cultural dynamics to illustrate how the Iranian and Arabic speaking contexts differ from that of the West in general and the USA in particular. We note the variations within the MENA region. This material sets the scene for how conflict emerges and is managed in the contexts in which BMBs live and worship.

2. Background Reflections on Discipleship: Conflict and Transformation

By Dr Roy Oksnevad

The Goal of Discipleship is Transformation

"Leading individuals to faith in Jesus Christ is the evangelistic dimension of mission. People come as they are, with their histories and cultures. We cannot expect an instant transformation of new converts' behaviour, beliefs, and worldviews. It is important, therefore, to disciple them into Christian maturity. This includes a transformation not only in the way people think and behave but also in their worldviews" (Hiebert, 2010: 12).

The Sermon on the Mount in Matthew 5-7 is a unique teaching of Jesus in which he challenges the disciples to stop the cycle of conflict, retribution, anger, and other sinful behaviour. The worldview that shapes cultural behaviour in North Africa, the Middle East, and Iran is honour/shame. Honour is to be preserved at all costs. Shame must be covered up, avenged, or removed. Honour killings are an extreme outcome of that worldview. In Western cultures, law or justice is the worldview that dictates how people are to be treated. Law and punishment in this worldview often override relationships; however, in honour/shame cultures relationships and cultural values shape the law and redefine justice.

When Jesus calls his believers to a higher standard, he confronts sacredly held cultural values and behaviours. Jesus taught his disciples on multiple occasions that he will be rejected, a man acquainted with sorrow, which comes from confronting the prevailing values of that day (Is. 53:3-4). Rejection is the first step of shame as per that culture. Jesus was clear that following him will cost them in every aspect of their lives. To be his followers, we are called to die to self (deny ourselves), take up the cross of Christ, and follow him (Lk. 9:21-26). To stop the cycle of sin, we must be ready to carry the shame and absorb the hatred and anger. To stop the cycle of honouring others to the point of miscommunication or injustice, Jesus calls us to say what we mean and mean what we say (Mt. 5:33-37). There is a cost in stopping the cycle of the behaviour of our culture, and for some, it is too costly. Jesus is calling us to count the cost in a continuous pattern of behaviour, that becomes a new culture itself. We are not implying some monocultural biblical culture, but one that is rich with cultural diversity. Using McGavran's imagery, we want to see every kindred and tongue will "beat all their 'swords' (meaning damaging cultural components) into 'plowshares', and all their 'spears' (meaning harmful customs) into 'pruning hooks'." (McGavran, 1974: 82).

God calls us to be a people set apart when he identifies us as a royal priesthood, a holy nation, a people unto God (1 Pet. 2:9), a transformed community that is salt and light to those around (Mt. 5:13-16). The world along with the principalities and powers of this world will resist this new community. The Apostle Paul encourages the New Testament Christians to put on the full armour of God to be able to stand their ground against the devil's schemes in living out this new community (Eph. 6:10-18). Paul reminds Timothy that to be a disciple of Jesus means to live a godly life. This Christ-like life will go against culturally acceptable standards which will result in persecution (2 Tim. 3:12). If we acquiesce to the culture around us, we cease to be the salt and light which God is calling us to be. We recognise that the first generation of believers in any context find it particularly hard to live out the Christian life counter-culturally. In addition, there are little to no support structures to strengthen the heart, emotions, and hands of those following Christ. The consultation sought an honest discussion on what it looks like to follow Christ and the challenges involved in cutting a new path that will not be understood by the majority of the people. We dared to discuss issues that are *haram* (forbidden) in order to disciple the new fellowships struggling to live out the gospel in a hostile environment. This book presents this daring and honest material to a wider audience in the hope and expectation that it will contribute to the development of healthy, vibrant fellowships in many contexts.

Guidelines for Transformation

The Bible is rich with stories of our failure through conflict as well as a guide in confronting conflict and sinful behaviour in a Godly manner. God disciplines those whom he loves (Heb. 12:5-11). God is forming a royal priesthood of believers to be salt and light in this world. Therefore, there is great wisdom to be mined in the Bible, looking critically at local behaviour, and charting a new course concerning how to understand conflict and how to overcome it. The tendency is to preach relevant Bible passages with the assumption that everyone knows how to apply the passages to their unique situation. It is more often the case that we preach the passage to address a conflict, but we rarely do the hard work of digging deeper into why we so readily gravitate toward self-defeating behaviour that we desire to change. The Bible should inform our discussions, but we must clarify exactly what must be addressed in conflict through the biblical lens.

In preaching or teaching the Bible, many evangelical preachers and exegetes propose three foundational principles that inform the message: a) exegesis of the scriptures; b) exegesis of our culture or context; and c) exegesis of the people to whom we are speaking. To the readers of this book, it is helpful to understand what Paul Hiebert calls critical contextualisation (Hiebert, 1987).

There are three main challenges affecting today's mission. First is the lack of inter-cultural understanding. During the middle of the 20th century, there was a shift from colonialism to what was termed postcolonialism. Postcolonialism viewed each society on its own terms, a good shift in perspective. Missionaries travelling to the mission field made the assumption that the nationals knew best. The problem with this perspective is that the historical contexts are largely ignored. It is true that each culture is to be understood on its own terms. But if that is the exclusive perspective, then there is no real communication between Christians in different cultures, no comparison between their theologies, and no common foundations of faith.

The second challenge is Guilt Complex. The postcolonial perspective has the tendency of creating what is called the trophy syndrome. The national worker is adored and can do no wrong. This is particularly true for pastors and other leaders who try to maintain their reputation and respect with others, while all the while their own personal devotional lives are dry and lacking in spiritual intimacy with God. Outsider Christians were sensitive to the historical legacy of colonialism, and therefore afraid to confront national leaders because of the Guilt Complex.

The third challenge is lack of missiological education. Majority of sending/mission societies around the world tend to live in a monocultural world that lacks skills in understanding other cultures. People assume that all behaviour within their society is normative or just the way things are. This created westernised Christianity in some communities within the MENA region.

Hiebert suggests a four-step process to open the door of communication between cultures:

Exegesis of the culture: Local church leaders and missionaries gather and analyse traditional beliefs and customs to understand the pre-Christian ways.

Exegesis of the Scripture and the hermeneutical bridge: In this step, church leaders and missionaries lead the church in a study of the scriptures to translate the biblical message into the cognitive (thinking or understanding), affective (feeling or attitudinal), and evaluative (skill or master) dimension of other cultures. The leader moves the people between the biblical culture and their own.

Critical response: In this stage, the people corporately evaluate critically their own past customs in the light of the new biblical understandings, and finally new contextualised practices. Some practices which affirm their cultural identity and heritage will be kept; others will be rejected because of hidden meanings and associations; some will be modified.

Critical contextualisation: This step does not operate from a monocultural perspective. BMBs are coming out of one culture (Islamic and national) into a new culture (Christian culture) with a different worldview. The Islamic or national culture should not be brought into the church's culture uncritically.

In line with Hiebert's four step process, we encouraged the presenters in the TTG consultation not to just quote scripture to address conflict. They were to do the hard work of exegesis of their cultural context and employ critical exegesis of the people in their fellowships to address the root worldviews that need changing. The presentations were followed by breakout sessions and a panel discussion to facilitate this critical exegesis of what is happening in fellowships/churches.

Culture's Influence on Behaviour in Conflict

Theologian Richard Niebuhr famously defined culture as consisting of "language, habits, ideas, beliefs, customs, social organisation, inherited artifacts, technical processes, and values" (Niebuhr, 1951: 32). The following is my contextual summary of Niebuhr's cultural heritage that impacts discipleship, conflict and transformation:

- People coming to faith in Christ bring their inherited cultural patterns of behaviour, as well as values that are shaped by their religion, culture, and family. These shape how conflict and forgiveness are expressed and addressed.
- BMBs come with little understanding of Christianity or how communities of Christians are expected to function in the midst of conflict. Since the BMB church is still in its early stages, the maturity of the Christians complicates the formation of healthy fellowships, particularly if there is no healthy Christian background church to assimilate into.
- Cultural hostility to conversion and familial pressure against conversion creates unavoidable and protracted conflict for most BMBs.
- Societies often develop characteristic emotional orientations. When people in a region experience intractable conflict, the protracted conflicts strongly shape their emotional makeup such that fear becomes the default emotional response in any kind of conflict.
- People who live with constant fear tend to misinterpret interpersonal cues and behaviours as signs of threat and danger. They unconsciously "see" the smallest hint of threat, even in situations where people are actually giving positive signals. This ingrained fear also leads to instinctive mistrust and misinterpretation of one who is perceived as an adversary. All these instinctual patterns make conflict messy and very hard to resolve.
- In fear-shaped societies, there is an "all or nothing" view of the conflict. Any giving in to the other's demands or views automatically brings into question one's interpretation of what has happened, of the conflict, and of the responsibility one holds for the past, present, and future.
- Typically, those who seek to bring about reconciliation or compromise spend a lot of time just trying to get people to stop reacting to one another out of fear and distrust, so that all parties in the conflict can listen to what is being said and meant.
- The victimisation common in totalitarian societies results in believers viewing themselves as victims and having a hard time trusting others. They can even struggle with discouragement and despair.

Understanding Conflict

Middle Eastern, North African and Iranian culture is highly sociable. This is reflected in the emphasis and value on how much time is spent together.

Paradoxically, these same fellowships struggle with interpersonal relationships which is the greatest challenge facing many of them. We will now take an in-depth look at cultural characteristics that contribute to the interpersonal struggles faced by the church.

Poor communication often leads to tensions whereby individuals quickly cross personal boundaries and hurt each another's feelings. Culturally shaped indirect communication styles create further tensions, fuelling gossip and speculation to fill in the information gaps. Mistrust also plays a part if the leaders have created a culture of fear and distrust of everyone. In such instances, rather than simply believing what people say, people have a tendency to assume hidden motives.

Some pastors/leaders do not communicate well, and they can also be competitive and unable to trust each other. Such limited cooperation, revenge-seeking, envy, criticism, and judgmental attitudes create an unhealthy environment. Once shamed, believers find it hard to forgive, especially for grave offenses. Never-ending attempts to get one's point across limit actual listening. Additionally, tensions between Christians from Christian and Muslim backgrounds create splits within Middle Eastern churches. Another complicating factor is that many cannot distinguish between a minor offense that can be simply overlooked and a major offense that needs to be dealt with.

Unfortunately, the emerging church is often not prepared or trained to deal with interpersonal conflict. Leaders typically hide conflict or deny its existence. Insensitive confrontation only leads to more conflict, often resulting in people leaving the church to escape the conflicts. Yet, forgiveness and reconciliation are foundational to the Christian life.

Conflict happens in every culture. Since people typically only seek to *manage* the conflict; reconciliation or resolution of conflict is rare. Interpersonal conflict, clashes over leadership and leadership styles, hypersensitivity over perceived offenses, and an inability to resolve conflicts are typical of a new church full of new Christians. Since few bring a strong healthy critically reflective cultural understanding of how to resolve conflict, many resort to their cultural default and deny the existence of conflict, try to control the conflict, or simply leave the church when conflict arises.

Lebanese American academic George Irani gives some helpful insights into how different cultures handle conflict resolution. "Western conflict resolution deals with definite, programmed, institutionalised relationships. Middle Eastern conflict is often unprogrammed, informal, and with random relationships" (Irani, 1999: 4).

To better understand how different various cultures approach the same subject, Mohammed Abu-Nimer, an expert on conflict resolution, charts the nuances between Western and Middle Eastern assumptions in conflict resolution (Abu-Nimer, 1996: 29-31). The intent of the following chart is not to uphold one culture over against another culture. Rather, it illustrates how different cultures approach the subject of conflict. While we might not agree on every aspect of Abu-Nimer's categorisation, it can be a helpful taxonomy.

Western Assumptions	Middle Eastern, North African and Iranian Assumptions
Conflict is positive	Conflict is negative and dangerous
Conflict is normal	Conflict should be avoided
Conflict can bring growth and creativity	Conflict brings destruction and disorder
Collaborative and cooperative frameworks are the essential components of conflict resolution	Group affiliation (family, clan, religion, sect, or other collective identity) is the most central and important identity that should be protected and sustained through conflict management processes
Facing a conflict is a necessary and recommended strategy	Spontaneous and emotional acts characterise Middle Eastern processes of conflict management, particularly in regard to the parties' interaction. Such behaviour is not only an integral part of the mediation and negotiation strategies, but it also reflects a strong characteristic of Arab society in general.
Since everything is based on regional reasoning, any conflict can be settled and managed through rational planning. Every Western conflict resolution model has four to twelve stages of intervention.	Social norms and values rather than legal forms are the main rules of commitment. Therefore, written agreements (or signing) are not part of the process. Instead, parties and third parties rely on established social and cultural values and norms in reaching and implementing the agreement.

Hofstede's Analysis of Middle Eastern Culture Tendencies[4]

Another helpful expert in intercultural research is Professor Geert Hofstede, whose comprehensive study on how values in the workplace are influenced by culture, is particularly useful to us. Professor Geert Hofstede conducted one of the most comprehensive studies of how values in the workplace are influenced by culture. Hofstede can be regarded as one of the leading representatives of intercultural research and studies. The findings of his research and his theoretical ideas are used worldwide in both psychology and management studies. He uses six values to measure the culture; they are Power Distance, Individualism/Collectivism, Masculinity/ Femininity, Uncertainty Avoidance, Long-Term Orientation, and Indulgence/Restraint. These cultural markers will help us understand the gravitational pull of certain characteristics that may be

---

[4] Hofstede Insights, "Country Comparison Tool", The Culture Factor Website, last updated: 16th October 2023. [Available at: https://www.theculturefactor.com/country-comparison-tool], [Last accessed: 6th June 2024].

found in BMB churches reflected in the six countries taken from Hofstede's country analysis focus.

It is important to note that 50 on the scale is the dividing line between the two expressions of the category. The higher or lower the number reflects how intensely the cultural expression is held. We also recognise that these are general cultural expressions and there are always exceptions within the geopolitical boundaries. The reason for choosing the countries including MENA and Iran reflects the people participating in the consultation. The USA was chosen to represent the dominant Western country that sends the most missionaries.

We might disagree with parts of Hofstede's taxonomy as we can notice some potential limitations in his research in what seems effectively to be a comparison between the MENA region and the United States.

Power Distance

Hofstede, in his research on global leadership, unpacks a cultural trait of power distance as the fact that all individuals in societies are not equal. The definition he uses for Power Distance is the extent to which the less powerful members of institutions and organisations within a country expect and accept that power is distributed unequally. In high power distant societies, employees are afraid of disagreeing with their boss and prefer for the boss to decide autocratically. They are dependent upon the boss. In low power distant countries, the employees are not afraid of the boss and prefer a consultative style of decision-making.

Egypt, Algeria, Morocco, Iraq, and Iran score high on this dimension (scores of 70, 80, 70, 95, and 58), which means that people accept a hierarchical order in which everybody has a place and which needs no further justification. Hierarchy in an organisation is seen as reflecting inherent inequalities, centralisation is popular, subordinates expect to be told what to do and the ideal boss is a benevolent autocrat.

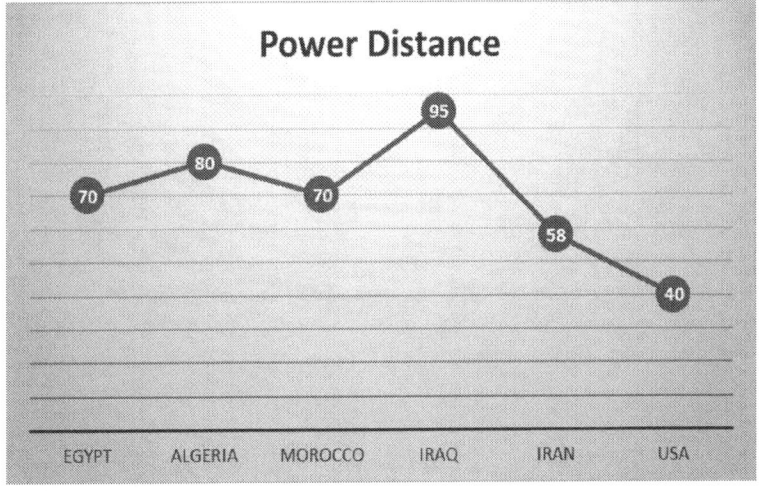

USA: The USA score was done differently. The fairly low score on Power Distance (40) is combined with Individualism in Hofstede's comparison. The USA is one of the most Individualistic (91) cultures in the world and reflects itself in the following way:

The American premise of "liberty and justice for all" is evidenced by an explicit emphasis on equal rights in all aspects of American society and government. Within American organisations, hierarchy is established for convenience, superiors are accessible, and managers rely on individual employees and teams for their expertise. Both managers and employees expect to be consulted and information is shared frequently. At the same time, communication is informal, direct, and participative to a degree. The society is loosely knit, in which the expectation is that people look after themselves and their immediate families only and should not rely (too much) on authorities for support. There is also a high degree of geographical mobility in the United States. Americans are the best at joining others in the world; however, it is often difficult, especially among men, to develop deep friendships. Americans are accustomed to doing business or interacting with people they don't know well. Therefore, Americans are not shy about approaching their prospective counterparts in order to obtain or seek information. In the business world, employees are expected to be self-reliant and display initiative. Also, within the exchange-based world of work, hiring, promotion, and decisions are based on merit or evidence of what one has done or can do.

Individualism/Collectivism

The fundamental issue addressed by this dimension is the degree of interdependence a society maintains among its members – whether people's self-image is defined in terms of "I" or "We". In individualist societies, people are only supposed to look after themselves and their immediate families. Individual interests override the interests of the group. In collectivist societies, people belong to "in groups" that take care of them in exchange for loyalty. Breaking loyalty is one of the worst things a person can do.

Egypt, Algeria, Morocco, Iraq, and Iran's scores (25, 35, 46, 30, and 41) are reflective of collectivistic societies. This is manifest in a close long-term commitment to the member "group", be that a family, extended family, or extended relationships. Loyalty in a collectivist culture is paramount and overrides most other societal rules and regulations. Society fosters strong relationships where everyone takes responsibility for fellow members of their group. In collectivist societies, offense leads to shame and loss of face, employer/employee relationships are perceived in moral terms (like a family link), hiring and promotion decisions take account of the employee's in-group, and management is the management of groups.

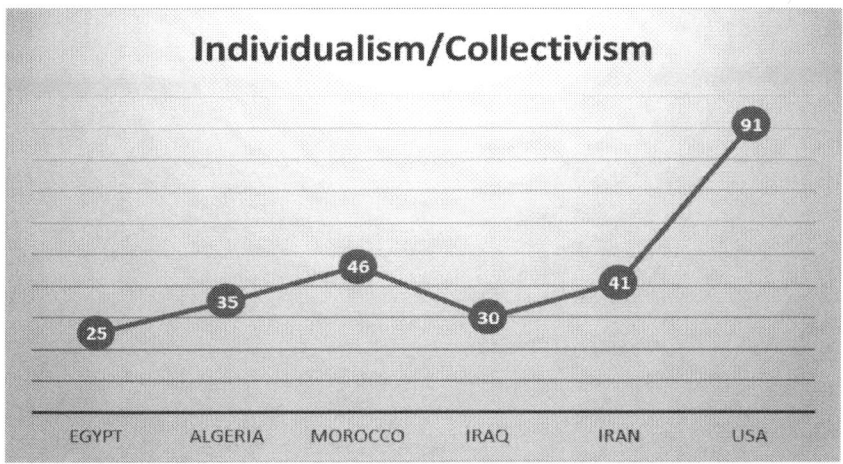

USA: This measurement was included in the Power Distance explanation above.

Masculinity/Femininity

A high score (masculine) on this dimension indicates that society will be driven by competition, achievement, and success, with success being defined by the winner / best in the field. This is a value system that starts in school and continues throughout organisational life.

A low score (feminine) on the dimension means that the dominant values in society are caring for others and quality of life. A feminine society is one where a good quality of life is the sign of success and standing out from the crowd is not admirable. The fundamental issue here is what motivates people, wanting to be the best (masculine) or liking what you do (feminine).

Egypt, Algeria, and Iran's scores (45, 35, and 43) place them in the dimension of a relatively feminine society. In feminine countries, the focus is on "working in order to live", managers strive for consensus, and people value equality, solidarity, and quality in their working lives. Conflicts are resolved by compromise and negotiation. Incentives such as free time and flexibility are favoured. The focus is on well-being; status is not shown. An effective manager is a supportive one, and decision-making is achieved through involvement.

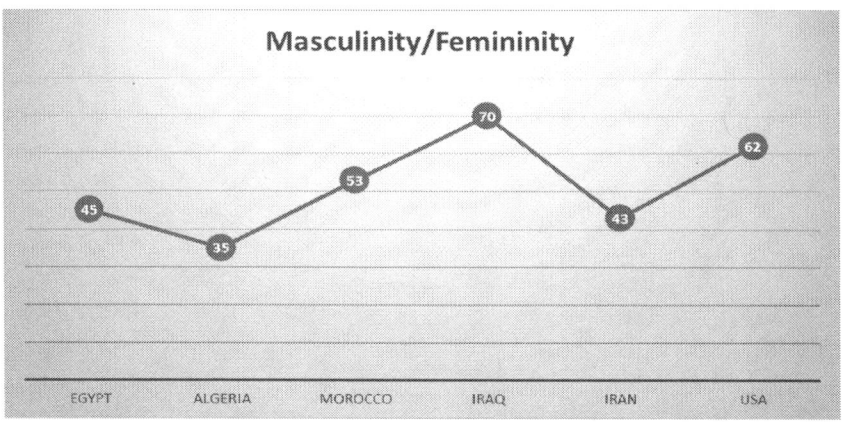

Morocco has an intermediate score of 53 on this dimension, which is inconclusive.

Iraq's score of 70 locates the country as a masculine society. In masculine countries, people "live in order to work", managers are expected to be decisive and assertive, the emphasis is on equity, competition, and performance, and conflicts are resolved by fighting them out.

USA: the score on masculinity is high at 62, which can be seen in the typical American behavioural patterns. This can be explained by the combination of a high masculinity drive together with the most individualist drive in the world. In other words, Americans, so to speak, all show their masculine drive individually.

Uncertainty Avoidance

The dimension of uncertainty avoidance is the way that a society deals with the fact that the future can never be known; should we try to control the future or just let it happen? This ambiguity brings with it anxiety and different cultures have learned to deal with this anxiety in different ways. The extent to which the members of a culture feel threatened by ambiguous or unknown situations and have created beliefs and institutions that try to avoid these is reflected in the score on uncertainty avoidance.

Egypt, Algeria, Morocco, Iraq, and Iran all score high or very high on this dimension and thus have a high preference for avoiding uncertainty (80, 70, 68, 85, and 59). Countries exhibiting high uncertainty avoidance maintain rigid codes of belief and behaviour and are intolerant of unorthodox behaviour and ideas. In these cultures, there is an emotional need for rules (even if the rules never seem to work), time is money, people have an inner urge to be busy and work hard, precision and punctuality are the norms, and innovation may be resisted. Security is an important element in individual motivation.

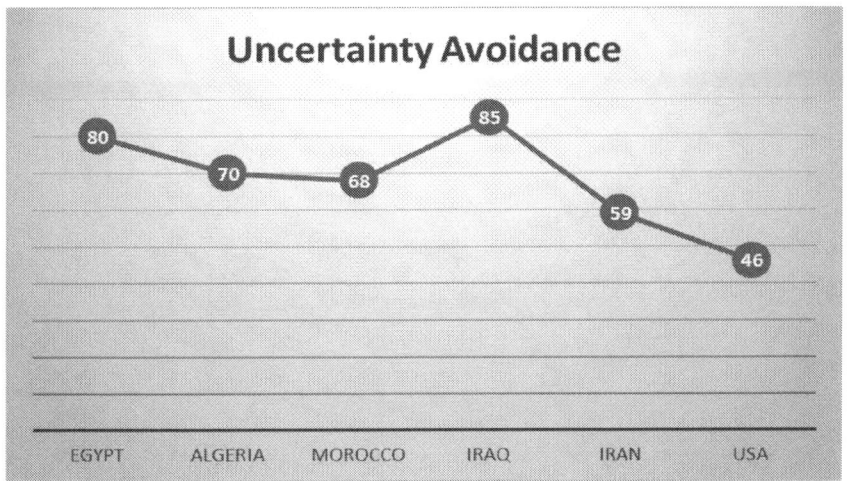

The US scores below average, with a low score of 46, on this dimension. Therefore, the perceived context in which Americans find themselves will impact their behaviour more than if the culture would have either scored higher or lower.

Consequently, there is a fair degree of acceptance of new ideas, innovative products, and a willingness to try something new or different, whether it pertains to technology, business practices, or food. Americans tend to be more tolerant of ideas or opinions from other people and they allow freedom of expression. Americans do not require a lot of rules and are less emotionally expressive than higher-scoring cultures.

Long-Term Orientation

Long-term orientation describes how every society has to maintain some links with its own past while dealing with the challenges of the present and future. Societies prioritise these two existential goals differently. Societies which score low on this dimension, for example, prefer to maintain time-honoured traditions and norms while viewing societal change with suspicion. Those with a culture that scores high take a more pragmatic approach: they encourage thrift or saving and efforts in modern education as a way to prepare for the future.

Egypt, Algeria, Morocco, Iraq, Iran, and the USA all score very low and low. The North African and Iranian cultures indicated that their cultures are very normative. People in such societies have a strong concern with establishing the absolute Truth; they are normative in their thinking. They exhibit great respect for traditions, a relatively small propensity to save for the future, and a focus on achieving quick results.

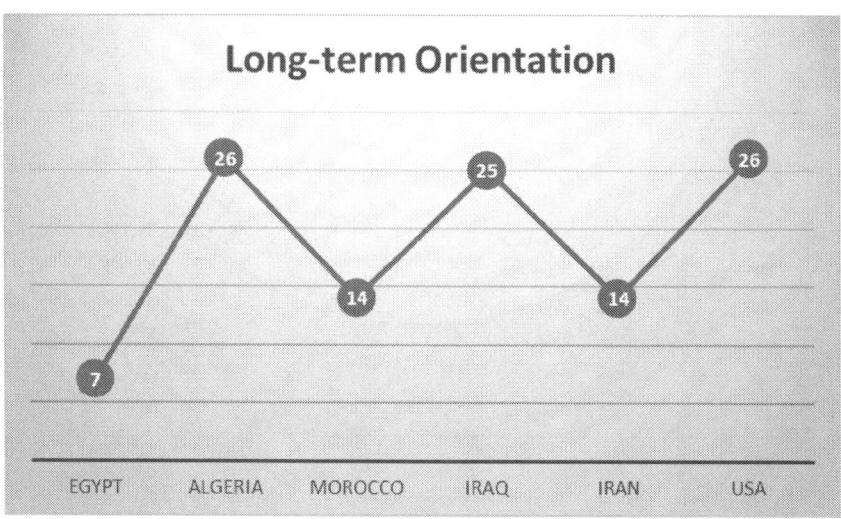

The US scores normative on the fifth dimension with a score of 26, but deserves special mention. Americans are prone to analyse new information to check whether it is true. Thus, the culture doesn't make most Americans pragmatic, but this should not be confused with the fact that Americans are very practical, being reflected by the "can-do" mentality mentioned earlier. The polarisation mentioned above is strengthened by the fact that many Americans have very strong ideas about what is "good" and "evil". This may concern issues such as abortion, the use of drugs, euthanasia, weapons, or the size and rights of the government versus the States and citizens. American businesses measure their performance on a short-term basis, with profit and loss statements being issued quarterly. This also drives individuals to strive for quick results within the workplace.

Indulgent/Restrained

One challenge that confronts humanity, now and in the past, is the degree to which small children are socialised. Without socialisation, we do not become "human". This dimension is defined as the extent to which people try to control their desires and impulses, based on the way they were raised. Relatively weak control is called "indulgence" and relatively strong control is called "restraint". Cultures can, therefore, be described as indulgent or restrained.

Egypt, Algeria, Morocco, and Iraq score from very low to low in the cultural dimension of indulgence (8, 32, 25, 17, and 40). This means that these countries are shown to be very restrained countries. Societies with a low score in this dimension have a tendency to cynicism and pessimism. In contrast to indulgent societies, restrained societies do not put much emphasis on leisure time and control the gratification of their desires. People with this orientation have the perception that their actions are restrained by social norms and feel that indulging themselves is somewhat wrong.

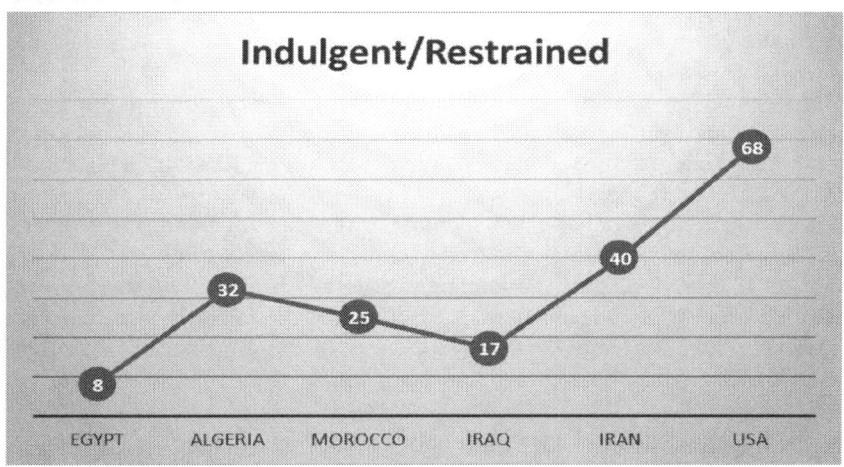

The US scores as an indulgent (68) society on the sixth dimension. This, in combination with a normative score, is reflected by the following contradictory attitudes and behaviour: work hard and play hard. The United States has waged a war against drugs and is still very busy in doing so, yet drug addiction is higher than in many other wealthy countries. It is a prudish society, yet even some well-known televangelists appear to be immoral.

Country	Power Distance	Individualism Collectivism	Masculinity Femininity	Uncertainty Avoidance	Long Term Orientation	Indulgent Restraint
Egypt	70	25	45	80	7	4
Algeria	80	35	35	70	26	32
Morocco	70	46	53	68	14	25
Iraq	95	30	70	85	25	17
Iran	58	41	43	49	14	40
USA	40	91	62	46	26	68

Cultural Trends to Watch

Culture, as defined previously, consists of language, habits, ideas, beliefs, customs, social organisation, inherited artifacts, technical processes, and values. Using the metrics above, we can expect to see many default values that these new churches and Christians will gravitate towards.

Under the rubric of power distance, we can expect the ideal pastor to be a benevolent autocrat but they can become less than ideal by becoming a toxic and controlling leader. A hierarchical governing structure will be put in place in the congregation and the members will expect to be told what to do. The pastor is expected to have more benefits which can lead to justification of more money from external sources, which can lead to conflict in the church.

In a collectivistic culture, churches will be loyal to family because loyalty overrides most other societal rules and regulations. Churches can become ingrown, with leadership given only to family or tribal members. Any offense leads to shame and loss of face. Leadership will be from within the pastor's in-group or family.

Since most of the countries fall into the feminine dimension, pastors will strive for consensus. Conflict is resolved by compromise and negotiation. Most will want to control the future since ambiguity brings anxiety with it. Therefore, they will want rules, even if the rules never seem to work. Innovation may be resisted. Security is an important element.

Since most countries in our focus score low in the long-term orientation, they prefer to maintain time-honoured traditions and view societal change with suspicion. They will tenaciously hold to absolute truth. This can be particularly delicate when the pastor is still relatively new in the faith as they may understand the faith in black and white terms. Coupled with a culture that naturally gravitates toward maintaining rigid codes of belief and behaviour, teaching and preaching is likely to become limited to the theological box the person has been instructed in. When someone in the church even considers another position, it can be viewed as allowing heresy to come into the church. Everything needs to fit into the small box that they understand, rather than the rich spectrum of Christian expressions and theology that comes with exposure to the worldwide church. Therefore, communication is stifled. In the dimension of indulgence, most score low, meaning they have a tendency toward cynicism and pessimism.

3. Communication:
Can We Just Say What We Mean?

Communication takes various forms. Some cultures use direct communication, while others use indirect communication. Both can cause conflict. Some expose everything no matter how offensive, while others sweep anything negative under the carpet, even to the point of denying its existence, to preserve face. Certain cultures want everyone to share their opinions since nothing is off-limits, while other cultures restrict communication about anything deemed dishonourable or taboo.

Cultural communication styles inevitably cause problems. Without good communication, the result can be gossip that fills the lack of transparency. Some cultural communication styles can leave people guessing what is really said. Iranians call this type of communication *taarof*: the dance one does to appear more genuine than one really is. Another communication style is so focused on getting their point across or preserving their honour, that the person doesn't really listen to what the other person is saying. The result is shouting at or past each other, since it seems that the chief goal in speaking is to get their point across, not listening first.

We can expect high power distant countries' cultural tendencies (Egypt, Algeria, Morocco, Iraq, and Iran) of communication to consider it normative that the pastor or person in authority tells the subordinates what to do or believe without further justification. In addition, a collectivist society will feel responsible for everyone else, so what someone wants to keep private will be made public, causing gossip and resulting in shame.

These cultural patterns of communication can be so engrained in people that the thought of another approach to communication would be considered alien. How do we overcome the problems associated with cultural communication styles in order to remove this aspect of conflict from our fellowships?

The first two presenters, an Iranian and a North African, were asked to make a recorded 20 minute presentation on the topic of communication to introduce the subject. What follows afterwards is the discussion that ensued from these first foundational presentations.

Conflict Through Communication – Iranian Presenter

I am Iranian holding degrees in both medicine and theology. I have ministered for over thirty years among Iranians, mainly as a bible teacher. I currently lead Elam's women's ministry which is playing an important role in shaping a culture in Iran's church where women are valued and honoured as equal members of the body of Christ. I have also authored two very popular books in Persian. I currently live in the UK, married with two grown up children, and two grandchildren.

A fictional case study: Pastor Hamid is a dynamic leader. With personal sacrifice, he successfully planted an Iranian church in a German city. Many Iranians attend, and there are conversions and baptisms, follow-up classes, and Bible studies. Pastor Hamid is popular. He enjoys what is normal in the Iranian culture – he is respected as an elder and teacher; the members are keen to show him loyalty, and they want to see his heroic pioneering qualities acted out in other scenarios.

However, over time, issues arise, such as around the way decisions are made. There is little or no discussion. Pastor Hamid's word is final. He has other commitments, remotely pastoring several churches in Iran and a TV ministry. So, Pastor Hamid is often not at the services. Members grumble that he never has time for them.

Tensions rise, but nobody wants to talk about the problems. These issues build up and, eventually, the church splits. Members start gossiping behind his back. Some feel that Pastor Hamid is being treated unfairly and are shocked by those who express criticism. Others think that his attitude is too high-handed. They have had enough. In the following turmoil, there is no reconciliation. Instead, there is an ugly split.

Ironically, the problems that contributed to the split are rooted in values that are very positive in Iran's culture: heroism, respect, and loyalty.

Iranians love to have a hero. This is true in politics; it is true in the church. The unwritten agreement between the hero and his followers is that the hero will always appear strong in public and will provide for his members. In return, the members will give back to the hero with unreserved respect and loyalty. Expectations are high on both sides. There is little space for constructive criticism of the leader. The pastor is to be respected and trusted. To question Pastor Hamid in public would have been disrespectful. Therefore, the issues in the church built up. Nobody wanted to talk. Everyone wanted to be seen as being loyal and supportive.

Most Iranians have been brought up in an emotional environment that is volatile and unpredictable. This gives people a default attitude of fear and caution. It is safer not to talk, as you do not know what the response will be. Moreover, a deep-seated pessimism reigns in the hearts of many Iranians when it comes to talking to a leader. They do not expect their opinion to be taken seriously; it is the person with power who usually wins. Talking will only make things worse.

Once the conflict is out in the open, it is often made worse by an assumption on either side that they know the motives of the other party. The opponents assume that there was an interest in power and money; the supporters assume his critics were interested in dragging down their hero. There is no room for discussion. Both sides want an unreserved apology and are ready to attack other people's characters.

Mediators act more like judges. There is no expectation of grey areas. One reason is that there is no teaching about conflict resolution in Iran's schools. The mediator is only brought in to add their voice to a judgement, not to help the parties decide how to resolve the conflict.

So the whole situation explodes and often there is a parting of the ways, rather than a resolution. Christians spiritualise this withdrawal by justifying that they have given this situation into the hand of the Lord, but often the real reason is helplessness or lack of determination to resolve the conflict.

The conflict could have been avoided if a church structure had been in place that ensured Pastor Hamid was accountable to a higher authority, such as a board of trustees or a bishop. The members had nowhere to take their misgivings, so there was silence until the explosion.

The answer is proper supervision of the pastor with accountability. Without that structure in place, any insistence on accountability can easily be interpreted as a lack of trust.

Western churches and their advisors can make a vital contribution to the future of Iranian churches. The Western church has many more years of experience in dealing with conflicts and an understanding that toxic issues cannot be left to fester. In the pioneering stage of the Iranian church, little attention has been given to the details of church government and organisation. Surely the time has come for Iranian church leaders to set up proper structures for all matters of church life – including an insistence that pastors be accountable, and that if conflicts arise there is a higher court where matters can be heard without bias.

Another practice that needs to be cemented into the structures of a healthy denomination is that of mentoring believers, which can be crucial in resolving conflict. Mentors can intervene before issues either accumulate or become malignant. The availability of mentors in discipleship and in the Christian organisational context can help resolve some issues before the conflict becomes irreversible.

Since the skills of conflict resolution are not usually taught in the Iranian culture, they should be intentionally taught, preached, and practised in the church with examples that are relevant to our Iranian culture. If this were included for new converts, they would be aware of what they should do when conflict arises, rather than reverting to the default answers of their own culture.

I have no doubt that the way forward is to act on these steps. Iranian Christians must set up structures of accountability, mentoring, and intentional teaching on conflict. The church will receive help from the experience of other churches. These structures will stand as a firewall against the ongoing tendency in our Iranian culture for issues to build up under the surface and then explode with devastating pain for all involved.

Good Communication Needed – North African Presenter

I am a native Algerian raised in a conservative Muslim family. After a successful career as a professional soccer player and manager, I joined Operation Mobilization in 1980 and have led its work in Algeria together with my wife since 1988. My wife and I minister through TV and radio, literature printing and distribution, sports ministry, and relief projects. Through the Timothy Training

School, we train workers for the Algerian churches and now for the nations. My wife and I have three daughters.

I have looked at this subject many times and sought for what the Lord may be giving me to share with you. One thing we must agree about is that, when there is silence, when there is no communication either within the church or between believers, then assumptions are made, and people start to imagine things. This is where the problems start when there is no clear communication. Therefore, it is so important to avoid all these assumptions and to communicate clearly with your people.

In Algeria, where we live, we are under the watchful eye of the government. We have experienced persecution for many years. This has intensified over the past two or three years, making it very difficult for us. The authorities have closed and sealed off many church buildings in Algeria, including the largest church in the country and the fourth largest in the Arab world.

In situations of intense persecution, communication is our lifeline. The first priority is to mobilise prayer among the believers in the country and among those beyond our borders. Second, we need to encourage believers to persevere and not give up doing ministry, even when our buildings are closed and believers are harassed. Third, our ministries must adapt to the changing situation in the country. All of this requires good and frequent clear communication. We continue to pray and fast, believing that God will intervene during this time of intense persecution.

On the positive side, constant and clear communication boosts morale. Through trying and difficult times, people need to be encouraged. Stories of God at work during daily life give believers hope to carry on. They need to hear throughout the week that God is with them. This gives them the courage to continue for the Lord. Doubts and fear can easily creep in but honest and truthful communication can clear away a lot of false assumptions and clarify some of the complex situations brothers and sisters are going through.

Relationships between brothers and sisters can easily become strained with poor communication and this can lead to tension and division. To avoid all this, we have to learn to communicate without fear and by God's grace to help us to be transparent.

Communication is key for church leaders and ministry teams. In so many instances, division could have been avoided if we had learned how to communicate well. Even if the leader is a poor communicator, if the people see our humility and brokenness, people would be encouraged and support their leaders. In our culture, it is culturally inappropriate to be so vulnerable as to cry in public. However, when I have not found the right words, I've been given tears by God. I have been able to communicate my heart through tears in these situations. Tears can communicate many things that words cannot communicate.

What Are the Main Basics of Communication?

In creating a culture of communication, the place to begin is with our communication with God. We must practice the presence of God by spending quality time with him. By so doing, we will learn to be sensitive to his voice and align our hearts with his. This intimacy and closeness with God will impact our communication style with others. God must reveal to us what he wants so we can share it with others. Depending on God brings renewal and the ability to mount up on the wings of eagles (Is. 40:28-31 and Phil. 4:13).

All too often, we end up depending on ourselves and on our own abilities and strengths, which leads to burnout. In these situations, our communication is only our own thoughts and our personal projects. Proverbs 3:5-6 admonishes us to "Trust in the Lord with all your heart and lean not on your own understanding; in all your ways submit to him, and he will make your paths straight."

In Algeria, we have many problems, such as divisions in our churches. Ministries have started well, but unfortunately ended badly. Leaders were not transparent and failed to communicate with the members of their ministry. Without transparency, assumptions are made to fill in the gaps of information. Gossip begins as believers begin to ask questions. The result is that the leader's integrity is questioned. Churches then split over loyalties. What is most concerning is that so many churches have completely dissolved, and members have dispersed. Leaders have kept information from the church, causing problems and divisions.

The vision that God has given our ministry is to bring others along to be part of the work with which we have been entrusted. From the onset of our ministry, we delegated the responsibilities and created departments. They are church planting, follow-up or discipleship, media ministry, and Timothy schools. Each department is headed up by a leader. Each leader has the freedom to seek God and develop the ministry within the umbrella of the House of Hope. It is our desire that each leader is able to own the vision, so they feel included on the team and responsible for their area of leadership. Communication and sharing responsibility are vital.

We found that a young man joining the team greatly desired to be a part of what God was doing. So I sat down with the young leader and I shared what God has in store for him through this ministry. It was during this time of trying to help this young man understand that I broke down and cried for him. I pleaded with him to not listen to the devil or walk according to the flesh, but be led by the Holy Spirit. This was a transforming moment for this brother and his life was transformed. He now is a key leader and others followed his example.

Finances, in particular, is an area that has been at the root of so many divisions. Ministries have failed because the leader was afraid to share with the believers where his money came from and how that money was used. Lack of transparency in finance leads to divisions among believers. To avoid all this, the leader has to learn to communicate and be very transparent.

Divisions can develop between members of the congregation. Leaders have a key role to play in communication and transparency. To be able to bring healing to the congregation, leaders must set an example through humility by listening to others and being willing to ask for forgiveness. The leader should teach and preach about humility, and they need to demonstrate brokenness and ask for forgiveness from others throughout their ministry. But if members don't see this modelled by their leaders, they will not learn humility, and the problems will continue unabated.

To illustrate what I mean, I will share another personal story. One of our brothers, along with his family, decided to leave our team because they believed that God had called them to another ministry. This hit me quite hard because he was an important member of my team. He shared what God had been teaching them. To demonstrate that they were not leaving because of a conflict, they wanted to wash our feet. It was a very moving situation. They asked for forgiveness for leaving the team. I was deeply moved by this act of love and humility. They left our team totally encouraged; we were inspired by their lives and their ministry and the way in which God is using them. This story demonstrates how vital communication is.

Here is a negative example of what can happen when not being transparent can ruin a good ministry. One of the main churches in this region has been an incredible blessing to so many. The church started in the late 1980s and early 90s. The ministry was built upon a solid foundation of memorising the Bible, fasting, and praying which were accompanied by signs and wonders. The church grew quickly. They had the heart to go out and preach. This fellowship planted another nine churches. They evangelised in the University, especially in Tizi-Ouzou and Kabila. Their ministry vision included doing evangelism in one of the main factories in the area where about 4000–5000 people were working. Those who converted went and shared the gospel with those in the surrounding villages and towns. God has used that church in amazing ways to spread the gospel.

Unfortunately, the leader was very authoritarian and was not transparent with the finances. He purchased a lot of material things for the church and soon the people wondered how he was able to pay for all these things. A meeting was called and judgements were made about him. The whole group was divided. Out of this ugly situation, some churches survived that were affiliated with the mother church, but others did not. Some churches separated and started other ministries, while others disbanded. It was very sad for me to see how God had used this brother in a very powerful way at the start, but how it had all unravelled. Poor communication, ego-centric authoritarian leadership, and not including others in leadership, caused many problems among the believers and led to his downfall. I think he has fully left the ministry.

If we fail to communicate clearly, we will fail to bring God's glory into our midst and in our ministries. Communication starts with our devotional time with God. It is in his presence that we learn to be humble and vulnerable. In addition, we need to learn to listen well so we can discern his voice. This is the foundation upon which we gain the ability to communicate with others.

Breakout Panel Discussion

A synopsis of breakout rooms is not possible since there was a technical problem with the breakout groups. Most breakout groups had trouble with the internet, not making discussion possible. The following is a reconstruction of one of the breakout groups and a representation of the discussion that ensued.

Authority Structures: I appreciate the first presentation. I have not seen a well-structured church in a Muslim context.

Our first speaker talked about authority structures and there were a number of comments in the chat saying this is an underdeveloped area. Is there resistance to developing structures for leaders? I am not talking about mentoring at this moment, but the church structures such as the board of elders, trustees, or bishop.

Responses: In my experience with North African brothers, there is such a culture of distrust that those who come to faith distrust each other. Trust is required for churches to have good enough relationships necessary to have a bishop or allow somebody to look into the lives of the leaders and to correct them when necessary. Even when a person is promoted into a position of leadership, there is still distrust. Ironically, there is more trust between a BMB and a Westerner, than between Tunisians, Algerians, and Moroccans. Even promoting a mature person into leadership who then has to balance other leaders on a board does not guarantee success. A person who knows more Bible verses is not necessarily a better teacher. The background these Muslims come from assumes that when someone has more Quranic knowledge, he is a better person. This attitude is brought into the church. So the more of the Bible one knows does not mean that their character is changed. The one who becomes the leader is the one who may have more head knowledge or who is physically more imposing. I have even seen that the one with the biggest living room is the pastor. This reality makes it difficult to build a church structure.

My experience in Egypt from the late 1980s to the early 2000s illustrates church structures. There was an attempt to build a structure with the local Christian background church, but issues of trust and personal insecurities made this difficult. The overarching political state realities in Egypt made any formalising of the structure difficult. We could agree on accountability, but it was never written on paper and formalised because that would create problems with security. On the one hand, we attempted to have that accountability and we had some informal structures in place, but still mistrust arose. It was easy for the Muslim background groups to opt out of accountability because they were disenfranchised from the Christian background believers. The informal accountability structures didn't resolve the underlying issues of personal insecurities, feeling threatened in leadership, and ownership of the group. Looking back, I think more intensive discipleship dealing with the inner personal issues and realising that these brothers had not been raised in a Christian family was what was needed. Christian families can be problematic; nevertheless, BMBs come new and fresh into the Christian environment and need to be brought in fully. The perennial issues that affect the willingness to come under accountability are basic humility, personal security, and self-worth. The accountability structure, mechanism, hierarchy, or institutional structure on its own won't create discipleship if people do not have intensive personal discipleship. They go hand-in-hand.

Western Fear of Helping: Westerners don't know how to handle BMBs believers and leaders. The church is happy to have them but lets them do whatever they want. In Switzerland, they are so happy to see Muslim background churches and members. They will have a department of Iranians, Afghans, and Arabs in numbers of 10-15 people, so the Westerners don't want to interfere. But we should provide help, disciple the leaders toward maturity and lead them by example. The unfortunate reality is a BMB becomes the chosen leader with no one alongside him to nurture him. Without this guidance, soon he is the assumed pastor/leader and he becomes prideful and unwilling to be challenged.

Talking Past Each Other: I saw two leaders in an Iranian church having a loud argument with one another after the church service. Their topic was speaking in tongues. As I listened, I turned to the man and said, "Ask her (the Bible teacher) if she speaks in tongues." Her argument was that God is great and he gives tongues to whomever he wills, that we can't limit God. The man was raised on the teachings of John MacArthur, who holds to the theological position of cessationism, that sign gifts are not for today. He was very much against having any charismatic theology coming into the church. Their argument continued for half an hour. The next day, I saw the man and he said he finally asked the Bible teacher if she spoke in tongues. He was surprised that, while she did not speak in tongues, she had room in her theology that God can give the gifts of tongues if he wants. Their heated debate of their own theological positions in the presence of church members illustrates uncontrolled communication, which encapsulates what happens in many churches. Communication is a learned art. The epistle of James says we are to be quick to listen and slow to speak (Jm. 1:19-20).

Communication and Discipleship: You grew up in Iran and now you have been living in Germany for many years. How much does that context influence discipleship in your community? Are the dynamics worse in Iran or is it the same in Iranian churches in Germany?

Answer: It is the same. We are coming from a culture of shame and honour and we do a lot of things in order to be accepted by the group. So when issues come up, we don't speak with each other about the problem because our need is acceptance.

What is the response when someone is challenged with a healthy way of dealing with communication? I am assuming that, out of the shame/honour or guilt/innocence categories in communication, Iran is more shame/honour. Is the response of the BMBs to a challenge in the way they communicate, "No you are just coming from a different culture, this is not our culture?" Or do BMBs say that there are no good or bad ways, but just different ways of approaching communication? How do Iranians respond?

Answer: BMBs want to be accepted by the other culture so they will not argue.

Communication Killers: Communication can be tricky. In the Iranian culture, whether you are Presbyterian or Pentecostal, there is a strong charismatic aspect to faith. I tried working with one young man who was a self-appointed pastor of a small Iranian fellowship. I started meeting with him to disciple him and saw the need to bring structure and accountability to the church where they met. One day, he came to my office and declared that he felt called by God to leave. He said that God told him that I was to be the next pastor. My response was God didn't tell me that. He was so convinced that this was God's leading that I couldn't talk to him. He left a few days later, which left the small church in confusion. Most stopped coming, but a few attended an American congregation. Six months later, the self-appointed pastor returned, declaring that God had anointed him to be the pastor of all Iranians in the area. This just caused greater confusion in the Iranian Christian community.

In an Arab fellowship which I attended, the BMB pastor met all the physical needs of the refugees, with the perspective that this service would obligate them to attend his services. He did not have enough time for discipleship and tried to pass off the responsibility of discipleship to other people who did not have the language or cultural skills for it. He wrote prayer letters giving glowing stories of what God was doing in his church. He would baptise people who had dreams of Jesus but also had dreams of Muhammad. He would say these people were Christians, and would take them with him to various churches to give their testimony of becoming a Christian. He would say that this was what God was doing through him. These people had obviously not come to Christ, because within a year they had left his church. I tried talking with him about discipling his people and learning if they were true Christians. However, he was working with a mainline denomination and the accountability team overseeing the ministry viewed him and his ministry as their trophy. Their perspective was to acquiesce to his leadership, since in their eyes, he knows the culture. They let him do the ministry and fully supported him in whatever he did. I asked the steering ministry team if any of them had ever done church planting. They said no. I tried to work alongside this Arab man for ten years, but finally withdrew.

Seemingly, a combination of several factors hindered our communication. Firstly, within Arab culture, the idea of an anointed leader, sheik or mullah, is the one who gives instruction, and will not be accountable to a wider group. The second is how to discern whether someone is mature enough or fit to lead.

Church Structures: As we see people coming to the US, we should be careful not to insist that they adapt to our American church ways. Let's find what works best in their own context. It is my opinion that we need to resist the temptation to draw former Muslims into our American churches. We shouldn't put them in the role of leadership and be in charge of ministries. Let's not parade them around as trophies. It seems that nothing good comes from that. Rather, we should encourage them to remain in their own community and explore what their faith looks like, starting with a house church model. Even though the house church is smaller, it would seem to work. I think that finding a like-minded group that is more culturally suitable, even economically, would be better for them. Westerners don't do life the same way other cultures do.

As a counter-argument, we are called by God to become a diverse church and express the diversity found in our communities. For a lot of Muslims I know, who have come to faith living in the UK, there is a desire to fully participate in the local church, which is more culturally diverse than a community made up of only Muslim background believers. We should be careful not to make them trophy conversions, but help them become full members of the church. They can bring their perspectives, insights, and experiences. We don't want to perpetuate a homogeneous expression of the church. We are starting to see multiculturalism here in the UK. There are many Iranians coming to faith, along with a small number of Afghans, Syrians, and North Africans. Some English churches that I know of have doubled in size through the presence of the Iranian community. It is massively challenging to the nature of what the church looks like. The cultural assumptions that we have are suddenly upended. It can be a bit chaotic when we are in transition, but it feels authentic.

As a Westerner who wants to help with BMB churches in some way, how can a Western church that is engaging with a Muslim background church or community avoid the two extremes? On the one hand, there is the fear of giving some help and guidance to address issues and health within the Muslim background church. On the other hand, there is the avoidance of trying to micromanage or format the church into its own image. Perhaps having someone who is a cross-cultural mediator who understands both cultures is the answer to avoiding the two extremes. Have you seen a Western church walk that tightrope well?

We have a video on our ministry's YouTube channel[5] in which we talk about the church within a church model. The worst one is what we call "the landlord model", which is hands-off involvement. When we were trying to get the Iranian church started, I met together with the pastors of both fellowships and I showed them the different models of multiple congregations. I asked them which one of the models represented what they were pursuing. They didn't have any idea. They guessed that they were a hybrid of two models. I asked which one they wanted to be. They pointed to the hybrid model, so I said that we should work toward it. But then the Iranian fellowship dissolved anyway, with God supposedly leading the Iranian pastor to another city. We have various models on our website, along with the strengths and weaknesses of each model.

The church that I am in is solely Iranian. Most Iranians want to be part of the Iranian community. It would be helpful for them to understand how the host culture and the Iranian community work. I, as an Iranian, have a difficult time understanding my own cultural dynamics because of the cultural part of communication that is called *taarof*. We say something but we don't mean it. It causes a lot of problems in the Iranian community. For someone from outside the community who doesn't understand the culture, it is very difficult to connect with the Iranian community. It is even difficult for me to understand my community, even as an Iranian.

---

[5] COMMA Network, "Church Within a Church: Models for multi-Cultural Churches", YouTube Video, Channel: COMMA Network, Uploaded: 14th February 2023, [Available at: https://youtu.be/WVuzkgEzBvw], [Last accessed: 9th September 2024].

Communication from the Outside: We had a BMB fellowship in the USA with people from several countries. It went really well for a couple years. We celebrated each person's culture and it was a place to disciple them. It was a rich fellowship. We gave them leadership and taught them how to do presentations and lead small groups. But there was a dynamic from outside this community of believers which affected us. The Moroccan community was attacking our Moroccans, saying that we were getting rich off of them by taking pictures and using them in our support raising. It was from people who were not a part of the fellowship and even Muslims saying these negative things. Finally, it destroyed the fellowship. As we debriefed a year later, the BMB leaders said they had no ability to respond to all the accusations that were levelled against them. They said that they were greatly influenced by the pressure of the outside ethnic community.

In the BMB fellowship that we had, it was people on the outside who assumed that they knew our motives. They projected these negative opinions upon us. It seems to be a part of the culture to assume and project hidden motives behind everything. To illustrate this tendency, recently, a Middle Eastern friend of mine was trying to read the hidden meaning of what a Western person said. My counsel to him was not to try to figure out the hidden meaning but take the comments at face value. Westerners generally mean what they say. If there is a hidden meaning, it will show itself. We should not read motives into what is said for it can start a problem where there isn't one.

We sometimes make too much about being Western and not being Middle Eastern in the way we communicate. The emotional skills of empathy and offering dignity to the other person goes a long way in covering the Western naivete in cross-cultural communication. It is possible to be a Western person, be very unaware of Middle Eastern cultural issues, and yet be very effective in ministry by being a sensitive, intuitive, and empathetic person. Such a person can become a trusted mediator. Sometimes, in my opinion, personal skills are more important than cross-cultural experience. I have seen people with many years of cross-cultural experience, who are still oblivious to the subtleties of cross-cultural communication. Having lived in a cross-cultural setting for twenty years doesn't necessarily make someone a great mediator or communicator.

Conclusion

Communication patterns we expect to see in a church fellowship are shaped by cultural values. Egypt, Algeria, Morocco, Iraq, and Iran all score high in power distance, meaning that churches will gravitate towards a hierarchical order in which the pastor is the unquestioned authority demanding loyalty from the members. Therefore, the less powerful, i.e. members of the congregation, confirm what the person in charge, the pastor or church leader, proposes. To go against these protocols can mean falling into disfavour with the leader. Communication patterns introduced from the West can cause confusion when the assumed rules in position and communication are questioned. Loyalty in a collective society takes precedence and overrides most other societal rules and regulations, meaning communication will seek to enforce loyalty with the pastor. The countries in our study are high in uncertainty avoidance, which complicates communication, meaning any ambiguous or unknown situations are to be avoided. Therefore, communication will maintain rigid codes of belief and be intolerant of unorthodox behaviour and ideas. This all-or-nothing way of communication will cause conflict when people of different church traditions and ideas try to voice their perspectives.

4. Honour and Shame: Living in the Shadows

Cross-cultural workers recognise that there are different cultural worldviews (guilt/innocence, honour/shame, and fear/power), which operate on different value systems. In humanity's fallen state, we tend to misuse our cultural worldview to our advantage. Islamic doctrine and practice institutionalise shame for anyone leaving Islam or who is not a follower of the religion of Islam. They are *dhimmi* (the term for non-Muslims living in an Islamic state and considered a protected subclass of people from which the majority extract payment), *kafirun* (a derogatory or shameful term for unbelievers; those who are not Muslims), or *murtadd* (normally translated as apostate; this is the most shameful term for one who turns away from Islam). These concepts are deeply entrenched in Muslim-majority countries and provide legitimacy for persecution or, in extreme instances, even death. Therefore, it is normal for parents and family members to use shame to try to manipulate a person who has become a Christian to return to Islam to remove the shame brought on the family through conversion.

These patterns of shaming behaviour are normative in cultures that rank high in the cultural expressions of collectivist societies, where everyone takes responsibility for the members of their family, tribe, or country. This is also exasperated when the cultural tendency is for uncertainty avoidance, where members of a culture feel threatened by unknown situations and have created beliefs and institutions that try to avoid differences in beliefs. Egypt, Algeria, Morocco, Iraq, and Iran all score high or very high in these categories.

Another aspect of shame is chronic shame, which is the ugly side of shame. The difference between shame and chronic shame is that shame can be positive if it is about something that was done, such as, "Shame on you, for not offering food to your guest." Chronic shame happens over a long period of time, which eventually impacts the very identity of the person. Some sources of chronic shame are psychological abuse, physical abuse, sexual abuse, financial abuse, and emotional abuse. Chronic shame is more intense and can last a lifetime, expressed as, "You will never be like your brother." "You will never get a job worthy of our family." *Chronic shame changes the perspective, so that the person is the problem, not their actions.* The result is that the person becomes hyper-sensitive, so even a neutral remark can be taken as a personal attack. Governments, religions, relatives, and family can abuse the individual so much that they struggle with self-worth. Chronic shame can be caused by an individual (such as physical or sexual abuse) or by the government or religion that abuses their people in order to control them and retain their position of power. In the latter case, an entire nation can become impaired in their functioning and mental health. Chronic shame is a source of conflict that must be understood as to how it impacts our fellowships.

People who are hurt or abused often hurt or abuse other people. So, we are to ask ourselves whether we end up chasing conflict, but rarely address the underlying cause of chronic shame? How do we overcome the problems associated with cultural shaming styles, removing this aspect of the conflict from our fellowships?

The first two presenters, an Iranian and a Middle Easterner, were asked to record a 20 minute presentation on the topic of shame to introduce the subject. What follows afterwards is the discussion that ensued from these first foundational presentations.

Honour and Shame: The Struggle to Live Up to an Invisible Standard – Iranian Presenter

I was born and raised in a Muslim family in Iran. Fifty years ago, Jesus called me to follow him. A few years later, I started the first Iranian church in the United States. Today, I pastor a virtual church among Iranians who are in Iran, Turkey, Armenia, Greece, Germany, England, and France. I am an author, speaker, teacher, and consultant at Shahzam Factor.[6]

I want to thank the committee who have given me this opportunity to explore this subject – honour and shame – one very close to my heart. It's a subject that I intimately understand because I have lived it all my life, which has motivated me to study it more closely.

I used to start my presentation by asking the following question: What causes a man or a woman to strap dynamite to himself or herself and blow himself or herself up? Then I would go on and answer the question, but I believe the following YouTube clip is much more appropriate since most of us Middle Easterners are not suicide bombers.

This is a video of Russell Peters, a Canadian Indian comedian, doing a parody on why Arab men can't say, "I don't know".[7]

What causes such behaviour? Some might call it a worldview. What is a worldview? God is the only person who knows the true worldview. The rest of us see reality through our own culturally coloured prisms. Worldview is that mental mapping of reality. Culture is created when we repeat that mental mapping of reality. The culture that dominates the Middle East is called honour and shame. Honour is avoiding shame at any cost. It is more valuable than life and makes life worth living. The desire to gain honour leads to anxiety and self-destruction, which is the mental mapping of reality.

Shame is a living hell and should be avoided at any cost. What created this culture of shame? Sin was the outcome when Adam and Eve disobeyed God, as

---

[6] https://shahzamfactor.com/welcome/.
[7] "Arab Men", A Clip from "Russell Peters – Notorious", YouTube video, Channel: Russell Peters, Uploaded: 1st November 2016. [Available at: https://www.youtube.com/watch?v=KCQwe_AMo74], [Last accessed: 9th September 2024]. This is an uncensored 6:41 minute video clip. The clip that was shown during the zoom conference was 5:26 and bad language was muted.

outlined in Genesis 3:7-10. What is the effect of sin? Guilt, shame, and fear are responses to sin, and they are the basic building blocks of every culture.

What is guilt? Guilt is that heavy emotional feeling we get when we do something wrong. It is the opposite of innocence. Guilt is shaped by an internalised moral ideal that doesn't need others to point it out to us. Historically, Western societal ways of measuring all moral behaviour are through the guilt versus innocence lens or worldview.

What is shame? Shame is the very heavy feeling that you are not measuring up to the established cultural standard. This expresses itself through self-loathing, not guilt. This feeling of shame is not for doing something wrong (the Western standard), but for being someone who is unable to measure up to what society wants you to be. It is the feeling of being unworthy, unacceptable, and naked before others.

What are the differences between guilt and shame? Guilt is related to what we do. Shame is who we are, which is inescapable. No culture is only in either a guilt or shame worldview. Like most things in this world, our lives are more complex, so these two worldviews often overlap. For example, one can feel guilty for lying to his mother and at the same time be ashamed for being such a son that would lie to his mother.

Not all shame societies are the same. Western shame is identified with the sense of unworthiness, which is more often rooted in some traumatic event. Western shame is seen through the psychological lens in which shame is considered as deeply internal. The way to treat Western shame is by building up the person's self-esteem so the person feels good about themself again. Middle Eastern shame is not necessarily caused by trauma, although it will cause trauma if left unaddressed. Middle Eastern shame is burdensome baggage that one carries from birth, and it is chronic or life-long. This shame is both interior, inadequate feelings from what we do or caused by a traumatic event, and exterior, imposed by society. A good word picture for shame is one in which the person marinates in the shame and can't escape it. Middle Eastern shame is failing to live up to cultural standards. The word we use in Farsi is *khaak bar sar-et* or "throw dirt on your head." It is another way of saying "you should die". We use that phrase to control or make people conform to what we want them to conform to. The opposite of Middle Eastern shame is honour which is getting society to think highly of the individual. In a desire to live up to the standards society has imposed on individuals, the person must keep honour at any cost. That is why we as Middle Easterners never confess failure or sin. When someone is caught not living up to the standards, the typical reaction is to blame others. It is shameful to admit weakness causing a lack of transparency in relationships about what goes on in our personal life. We try our best to maintain the image of honour.

The domino effect of keeping honour at any cost is a lack of trust. The attitude of holding honour at any cost is reflected in the focus of comparing ourselves with others. This leads to tearing down anyone who might be more successful than we are through the vehicle of gossip. Using a Western phrase, we never[8] "air out our dirty laundry" to outsiders, or we never reveal personal matters in public which should probably be left private. In addition, keeping honour at any cost brings with it high expectations of each other, a lack of forgiveness, a culture of lying and cheating, and using flattery and gift-giving to present an honourable image in public.

Solutions: What are some of the key solutions to Middle Eastern shame when dealing with BMBs? When dealing with people like myself, it is important to realise that I may have come out of Islam, but Islam has not come out of me. Using the Old Testament illustration when God instructed the Israelites when entering the promised land, "You must not do as they do in Egypt, where you used to live, and you must not do as they do in the land of Canaan, where I am bringing you. Do not follow their practices" (Lev. 18:3). Israel came out of Egypt, but the first generation still reflected the Egyptian mentality in them. I call this Post Traumatic Shame Disorder.[9]

Another solution in dealing with Iranian Muslim background believers is the need to gain their trust through transparency, admitting weaknesses and failures openly. Instead of trying to have an answer to every question, admit when you don't know the answer. It is important to embrace weakness as a gift of levelling the field as humans who are not omnipotent. This can be achieved by not lording yourself over others through using titles but by treating others as peers. These subtleties are very tricky to navigate, so we should be aware of them to understand where former Muslims are coming from. On the other hand, we are commanded by Jesus to make disciples. There must be accountability when making disciples, but as the discipler, you will have to model transparency, admitting weaknesses and failure openly.

Conflict from a Shame Culture – Middle Eastern Presenter

I am from the Middle East and I want to share about conflict from a chronic shame perspective. I will be presenting shame from the Middle East and North Africa region, some Eastern cultures, and parts of Asia. I will begin with an illustration. In the West, the law says we cannot go through a red light, so you stop at the red light no matter whether it is day or night. That's an illustration of guilt culture. An illustration of shame culture is when we look around and, if there is no policeman or anyone watching, we go through the red light. If people don't see us, it is considered ok.

I am generalising, but in a shame/honour culture, we look through the lens of how others might perceive us. We all want to be honoured; therefore, we don't want to do anything that would be perceived as dishonourable or shameful. Avoiding the perception of shame is part of what we must deal with living in a shame culture.

---

[8] Middle Easterners often express themselves in extremes to show either the truthfulness of their argument or to emphasis a point.

[9] Shahrokh Afshar would like you to credit him if you ever use this version of PTSD; the more common usage of PTSD is Post Traumatic Stress Disorder.

The Impact of Shame

Shame has an impact on us which can be negative, positive, or devious. Shame causes us to experience feelings of abandonment, withdrawal from society, isolation, and self-blame. A shamed person might believe he is shameful and have feelings of self-pity, or victimisation. To counter this feeling of shame, we walk around with a sense of false humility or false pride to cover the shame we feel. As former Muslims, we grew up shaming the minority Christians in our community by calling them names and calling their religious beliefs into question. We shamed Christians by saying they don't smell good, they were *kufirs*, and they were ugly. We tend to shame Christians because they were minorities.

From a shame culture perspective, we are conscious to do everything to cover our shame or in some extreme situations, to remove the shame by killing someone (honour killing). Honour is such an important value that we would do anything to protect our honour and to stay away from shame. Therefore, lying to protect our honour is considered a positive value.

When you lose your honour and are put to shame, two main things are affected:
1. The identity which is shaped by the family and community you grew up in will be affected. You experience a loss of the value that your people give you. For example, one person shared how his opinion as a Muslim used to be important in his community, but now as a Christian, he feels he has no value within his own family or society.
2. Shame is often accompanied by fear. For example, in Genesis 3 after Adam sinned, he felt shame and hid in the garden. He hid from God because the shame and disobedience he experienced produced fear. So much of the Bible takes place in the Middle East and has many similarities with our present Middle Eastern culture.

Another dimension of shame is when conflict arises. The natural response is wanting to seek vengeance. A lesson God taught me was to forgive the ones who sinned against me and make my heart clean in front of him. It took two years to learn how to get over the hurt I experienced. It is important to let God heal our deep feelings of shame. God knows all the painful details we have gone through. As Psalms 139 instructs us, God knows us intimately and we don't need to be afraid or ashamed of being in his presence.

An important perspective is to remember that all people are made in the image of God. We have to give others honour, even more than the honour we have. We don't need to expose them or display their dirty laundry. We are all sinners. We are responsible and accountable before God.

The Bible is replete with images of shame. When Adam sinned, God covered his sin with animal skin which points to the day of forgiveness in the Old Testament. When Noah was naked, his sons walked backward to cover Noah's shame and nakedness, for it was shameful for someone to be naked in front of others. In the New Testament, Joseph the carpenter didn't want to expose Mary to shame with her pregnancy before marriage, which could have led to her stoning, as per Jewish traditions. My mother's constant prayer for me was that

God would cover me; it is a metaphor for God's cover for our sins. When Jesus died for us, he covered the shame of our sin. As the Bible says, Jesus endured the shame of the cross (Heb. 12:2). We all are steeped in shame because of sin, but the real honour is how we will stand before God, cleansed from our sin and shame.

What is the response to our shame? Confession and repentance are the keys. First, we need to repent from the sin we have done to our brother/sister because they are created in the image of God. Second, we need to respond with forgiveness instead of responding with the cultural default setting of vengeance or an eye for justice. Third, we must learn to forgive the ones who hurt us. Christians are to be honourable, and we do this when we forgive and honour others. Growing up in the Middle East, we used to say "blood never becomes water", but when I became a Christian, I was angry at my family because they were ashamed of me. I had to forgive them for this betrayal. As I grew in the maturity of my new faith, I realised they carried shame because of my conversion to Christ. Remember, it is not always about what people did to us but also what I have done to them. We need to cover each other's shame. Christ calls us to love others more than ourselves, which means we need to repent of what we have done to others. Christ is our example. He died for us, losing his honour by dying the shameful death of the cross in order to give us honour in our relationship with him.

Discussions on Chronic Shame: the Challenges

The following represents the panel discussions on the topic of shame in the Middle Eastern context. The material is presented as challenges followed by suggested solutions.

Chronic shame is such a deep issue. It almost feels overwhelming. The first generation will wrestle with shame, but the second generation will have greater freedom from chronic shame.

The Complexity of Shame is Multi-Layered: There is a cost involved in humbling yourself in the eyes of others. An example of this is from an Arab pastor faced with the possibility of losing the people who were coming if he didn't meet the people's expectations of him. The relationship was complicated because he was providing for their needs. Most of those attending his services had not become Christians. So, from his perspective, he couldn't go against the cultural norms that were a part of the honour/shame culture. The cost was too high for him in the eyes of those with whom he was working since the people attending were not playing by the same rules.

We realised that the conversation turned to discussing the cost of being a disciple of Jesus. It was suggested that we should be talking about the gain we have in Christ instead of the cost. The late Coptic priest, Abouna Makary, talked a lot about what we gain in Christ. The challenge is that Jesus said we will lose our father, mother, brother, and sister but we also gain others (e.g. Mt. 19:29; Mk. 10:29). The challenge for us in the church more generally is whether the experience and the reality of our life together in the body of Christ really reflects a new surrogate family that someone would want to be part of. If the church is only defined as individuals who get together to have a really good time on Sunday for worship, but we all go home and have our individual lives from Monday to Saturday, that is not very attractive for someone who has come out of a culture where they love their mother, father, and family. Are they willing to lose all of these relationships and live with the shame associated with coming to Christ and the honour of being with this new community of God's people?

Shame and Honour Can Be Positive or Negative: Jesus lived in a shame and honour culture. Shame and honour are not negative; they can be wonderful, positive, and liberating characteristics. The point is, in what do we find our shame, and in what do we find our honour? Is our honour in our person, which is egotistical, or is it more in our relationship with Christ and following him? People coming out of honour/shame cultures have a lot to offer globally. They have just as much to contribute to the global body of Christ as someone who comes from a Western or guilt/innocent culture. There are positive and negative elements in every culture. BMBs have given up a lot in terms of family, belonging, and identity, and have shifted their identity to the body of Christ. The body of Christ needs to show itself worthy of those who have given up so much to follow Christ. We do that by honouring those who have lost family and being an alternative family to them. We are not asking the honour/shame person to mitigate their loss, but we also need to realise that the church operating in an honour/shame culture should greatly honour the dignity of these persons and the cost that they pay.

It was recognised that many of these BMBs live within their own communities, all Iranian or all Arab churches, and are not looking to the broader community, such as the church in the West. They are experiencing church within their own culture and want honour among their peers; to do that, they must become servants. That tips their whole value system upside down. This is not automatic upon conversion since the disciples never understood servanthood until after Jesus ascended and the Holy Spirit was given. Even after Pentecost, the disciples struggled with living out servanthood.

A dimension only hinted at during the discussions was the impact of *dhimmi* status on Christians coming out of Islam. This is a status of shame. Islam places anyone leaving Islam into a legal category of shame. In response, Middle Eastern followers of Christ express their identity with pictures of martyrs in churches and homes. To be a martyr is something absolutely natural and part of their identity. These martyrs are their role models, and it isn't through riches or material things, but being a martyr is a way of gaining eternal glory. Is that a way for Muslim background believers to deal with their shame?

Another perspective of honour and shame comes from living in a glocal (global/local) world. After the COVID-19 pandemic, many churches by necessity have gone online. The prominent ones are the mega-churches and they present an image of a worship service that is very appealing. There is a growing trend of mega-churches becoming their own sending agency and along with them comes their money which is highly coveted. This presents an image of high honour and the emerging BMB church wants to emulate what they see online.

We are now in a global village as well as the local world where people live, which brings with it its own set of problems and opportunities.

Another slant is that we, as the church in the West, have honoured things that are not the core of Christian honour. We honour power, prestige, big pulpit, high people, and numbers. Part of the problem is that, in the West, we have communicated a message implicitly or explicitly that certain things are honourable, and those things have very little to do with following Jesus in true biblical faith. These BMBs are stepping into a confusing world which is difficult to navigate.

Discussions on Chronic Shame: Solutions

Modelling Transparency: The gospel and faith are best transmitted from person to person. Leaders or influencers in the Middle East need to model that we are under the authority and in submission to the leadership of the global church. We need to model how we receive correction and openly talk about how we have to be corrected. I have often shared with my Arab brothers and sisters how I have changed in my marriage over the years. I realised that I did things that were stupid. I was prideful, arrogant, and authoritarian over my wife. All those things had to be radically shifted. Just modelling that kind of transparency as non-Arab or non-Iranian witnesses is important.

Talk About the Cost: Not everything is positive when coming to Christ. There is loss and sacrifice and that is an honourable thing. Christ-shaped honour looks different from cultural norms, for it comes with loss. We, especially BMBs, need to be honest about the losses we suffered for obedience to Christ and there is real joy in doing that as well. People need to see this mature response to be able to share in it. Modelling is the key.

Modelling our Identity in Christ: Our dignity is found in modelling our identity in the *Imago Dei*, being created in the image of God. First, our identity is found in Christ. Second, following Christ involves picking up our cross and following Jesus all the way through to the resurrection. Jesus is the crucified one.

Modelling Through Forgiveness: Asking for forgiveness for offenses that are not huge goes a long way. Most have not had or seen what a true friend looks like which is modelling honest feelings and being real. It is not shameful. We should model Christ-like character by not lingering with feelings of shame, but showing how we take those feelings to Jesus. By modelling our transparency, we are showing BMBs what it means to have our identity in Christ, which is honourable.

Develop a Learning Community: It is also important to find those who have a heart which says, "I need to learn more." It is a good indication that they are overcoming their shameful past. These are the people we should be looking for to help mould true Christian leadership. With Jesus, anything is possible, but for us now it feels overwhelming.

Focus on Christ: The best experience I had in conflict resolution was when I turned the conversation away from the people themselves to Christ. We can simply ask, "Let's look at Christ and what he did." Changing the conversation taken is wrong. We have seen that many self-appointed pastors forbid members from attending another fellowship. How do we overcome the problems and conflicts associated with such cultural leadership styles that try to control their fellowships?

Two presenters, a Middle Easterner and an Iranian, were asked to make a recorded 20-minute presentation on the topic of toxic leadership to introduce the subject. What follows afterwards is the discussion that ensued from these first foundational presentations.

Conflict from Toxic Leaders – Middle Eastern Presenter

I am an ordained minister and served in a church for thirteen years as a senior pastor. I, along with other like-minded leaders, have been instrumental in overseeing a church planting movement and my church as a catalyst church. I still maintain a role within the leadership of the churches. I have also worked extensively in the areas of peace and reconciliation.

It is difficult to live in an atmosphere of toxic leadership. Toxic leadership has to do with how leaders relate to others. It is an attitude. It is how you think about yourself and how you view yourself in regard to others.

How can we avoid toxic leadership? How can we avoid being a leader who views himself as God over the ones around him? The solution is clear, and we have it in the word of God. We have to be aware and consider if we have a superior attitude thinking that we are above others. We need to be careful as leaders, especially if we have leadership gifts to influence others. Leaders offer themselves in service, which is a very positive Christian act at its core. Jesus is the ideal leader for he was called the good shepherd. As a good shepherd, he offered his own life on the cross. We can learn from Jesus how not to be toxic leaders.

What do people feel about toxic leaders? The majority of people who are around toxic leaders feel fear. Toxic leaders have authority over people who allow them to make changes, whether positive or negative. It is wrong to misuse the authority that is given to us as leaders.

The culture that believers from a Muslim background come from is often one filled with fear. This arises from authoritarian leaders who controlled their people with oppressive rules and a religion that dominated the people. They also have feelings of guilt and shame living in a shame/honour culture that shapes how they live. When they follow the Lord, they bring with them this history of living in a culture that was very difficult for thirty or forty years. It was dominated by fear and shame which leaders misused for authority. This history is projected onto the church community. What is needed is to get these patterns changed. We use discipleship as a tool for transformation and getting over such negative factors that believers picked up from their own culture before following Jesus. It is important to put biblical culture before anything else. We can get rid of toxic leadership through true discipleship and following Jesus' leadership example.

---

away from their emotions puts distance away from the immediate. When we talk about Christ, things seem to just clear up. They become more transparent. Jesus' life is very straight in how he deals with this. This is the most powerful way of bringing change in the immediate situation.

Have a Long-Term Perspective of Transformation: This example was shared when talking about these complicated issues of chronic shame. I was a pioneer church planter in the inner city in very poor districts in the NY/NJ area. The church planting committee wanted every new church to become self-supporting, self-governing, and self-propagating within 3-5 years. Instead of thinking 3-5 years, I suggested thinking 3-5 generations. If you can stop the downward spiral in the first generation, it is the power of the gospel that transforms people. Then you work with the second generation, but they have already been deeply scarred by the first generation's values and habits. The church becomes the surrogate parent of that second generation showing a new way to live. Then, Lord willing, out of the union of a Christian marriage of the second generation will come a third generation who will become the mature leaders of the church. This process can happen in the first generation but that is not the norm. Transforming a worldview is a process that takes several generations to reformat. It is not easy. There is a cost. We must embrace its struggle and we need to talk about it. Not everyone is willing to pay the price, particularly under the heavy pressure of the family and community, or based on their insecurities. This will be part of our ministry with the first generation. We don't have to complain about it. It is helpful to have a long-term perspective of ministry in the back of our minds.

Resources: In the course Joining the Family, there are interviews with believers from Muslim backgrounds (Iranian, Pakistani, and others) about their experience of integrating into Western churches. It is a helpful course that takes into consideration the issues BMBs face (https://www.joiningthefamily.org/the-course/). Tim Green has done a lot of good work in the context of working in honour/shame communities.

Conclusion

Honour and the preservation of honour is one of the dominating forces of people growing up in an honour/shame culture. The honour of the family is dependent upon conforming to the standards laid out by the family, clan, locality, culture, and religion. Both of our presenters expressed shame in very personal terms as the heavy feeling of not measuring up to the established cultural standard. It brings with it the feeling of being unworthy, unacceptable, and naked.

The countries represented in our consultation scored as collectivist societies in Hofstede's study affirming that shame is a cultural value. However, our presenters admitted that Middle Eastern shame is burdensome baggage from birth, and it is lifelong. A shamed person's very identity is affected, particularly when they become a Christian. They lose their value in the eyes of others. Fear also accompanies shame. Responses are many – from feelings of abandonment, withdrawal from society, isolation, and self-blame. The natural response is to seek vengeance on those who shamed someone to restore some sense of honour.

The consensus was that the first generation will wrestle with shame, but the second generation will have greater freedom from chronic shame.

The solutions presented by the keynote presenters were insightful. First was a long-term look at the impact shame culture has on the person. Although a person has left Islam and come to Christ, Islam has not completely come out of the first generation, an allusion to Leviticus 18:3. The first generation struggles with the residual effects of shame. The second solution was also a theme that showed up in the other presentation: modelling transparency or embracing weakness and failures openly. Discipleship should be included from the very beginning, learning that it is not shameful to admit that you do not have all the answers and to stop pretending to know everything. Third, the response to shame should be forgiveness and not the default setting of vengeance. Fourth, we need to learn to forgive the ones who hurt us. Jesus is our example of forgiveness at the shame of the cross. In addition, the Bible is replete with images of shame that can speak to our culture.

The discussion groups revealed that shame is complex, but there were several ways of looking at it. Shame can be positive or negative depending on your perspective. Many BMBs have lost face with their family and community through the shame of the cross. It is important for church leaders to share honestly about the cost of following Christ, but also share a mature response, focused on Christ who endured the cross, scorning its shame and fixing our eyes on Jesus (Heb. 12). We should model honest feelings, but not linger on these feelings. Our identity is in Christ, his church, and the Christian community of believers.

5. Conflict from Toxic Leadership: "Someone Needs to Control the People"

Some cultures come from an egalitarian perspective in which every[one is] considered equal. Others come from cultures in which status and positi[on are] understood in a defined hierarchy. Both are different ways of appro[aching] leadership. In many cultures, there is a long history of political or rel[igious] leadership that has used power to squelch dissentient voices and impos[e their] will upon the people.

Drawing upon the insights of Geert Hofstede noted in Chapter [1, the] combination of high power distance (people expect that there is an u[nequal] distribution of power), coupled with high uncertainty avoidance (main[taining] rigid codes of conduct and intolerance of unorthodox behaviour and idea[s), and] ranking as a restrained society (where the powerful restrain or contro[l those] under them), there is a cultural pull to accept strong authoritarian leader[s who] in turn control their members. Is it possible that these patterns of gove[rnance] have invaded church polity, resulting in an authoritarian or dictatorial f[orm of] leadership? In this system, the role of the leader is to provide for those [under] his/her/their care. In response, those who benefit from the leade[r give] him/her/them their unquestioned loyalty. The cultural pattern is that restr[aint is] imposed from those in power (or outside the individual or society) instead [of the] biblical model in which the Holy Spirit restrains behaviour from the ins[ide. It] will take time to move both leaders and church members to the biblical m[odel.]

Two dimensions of this topic need to be considered. First is the r[ole an] abusive and autocratic leader plays in the conflict experienced in the c[hurch.] Second is the role of the members of the church who desire and expect the [leader] to be a strong man to control them and to tell them what to believe[. Both] dimensions must be addressed, for both are complicit in the conflicts that [arise.]

It has been observed that church fellowships grow during the "honey[moon] stage" of a church's life but, when conflict comes, the leadership tend[s to] reveal themselves. The human tendency is to draw upon the style of lead[ership] they are familiar with. For example, if the pastor or church leader had an a[utocratic] father or clan patriarch, in a crisis, he tends to draw on a familiar way of d[ealing] with problems. Even if the outcome was less than ideal, at least they are fa[miliar] with the process. Using a different way of dealing with conflict can be da[ngerous] for they have gone beyond the rules they are familiar with. These leaders [expect] unquestioned loyalty and compliance with the will of the leader. T[his is] complicated even more by any emotional insecurity, lack of experien[ce, or] inadequate training the leader may have. The result can produce rigid[ity,] holding on to their position, even if it is obvious that the position the lead[er]

Toxic leadership comes with different challenges, especially in the Middle Eastern context. I pastored churches for many years, and I was a senior pastor for a church in Jerusalem. I am an Arab-Palestinian pastor. After I had my personal encounter with Christ, the Lord brought me to a small congregation which shares all the common challenges of churches around the globe. One conflict concerned one of our leaders who was overwhelmed with other ministries because he didn't delegate as he should. When he was confronted, his reaction was aggressive which led to a traumatic split in the church. Many people were affected by this conflict and the reaction in the church was animosity toward the leaders. Despite all the mediation trials, many members kept to their decision of leaving the church for good. Those who stayed who were part of the conflict were viewed with suspicion by the rest of the congregation. Ten years later, when I became the pastor, I tried to empower my leaders from the new generation. A few old leaders were intimidated by my leadership style, and the old resentments raised their ugly heads but were less aggressive this time. There wasn't a public display of anger, but I received many notes of rejection, and some leaders even left the church. I felt threatened and attacked as a leader. It was difficult for me, and I tried to restore the relationships but, for some, it was too late. I felt I was not treated justly. I cannot deny that some of my reactions were toxic or unhealthy. I needed someone to talk to and sought outside help. I felt insecure, that maybe I was not a good leader. I was hurt badly, and I needed healing.

I advise anyone who goes through a similar experience, to seek help from mentors who are more experienced and older. Seek counselling where you can share your feelings and have people pray for you. Their insights will guide you on the best way through your challenges in leadership. For churches in the Middle Eastern, like those in any other context, experience of conflict often splits them. In my travels, I noticed that churches have similar conflicts to ours. In most of these cases, I highly recommend getting external help, such as an organisation or advisors who can build bridges to resolve conflicts. In the case of a church split, the two parties in the conflict should separate on good terms with an agreement between them. I would advise bringing groups or certain ministries specialising in trauma healing to repair the broken relationships. Should you do this, the light of Christ will shine on you and help the ministry to be restored.

My Journey with Abusive and Toxic Leadership – Iranian Perspective

It is truly an honour for me to be invited to contribute to this important subject. I appreciate anytime we gather to discuss issues of discipleship among the Christian communities from Muslim backgrounds because these themes are very near and dear to my heart. I hope that these discussions will help us to grow in our understanding of how best to disciple, train, and equip the growing movement to Christ in the Islamic world. I speak from the context of the Iranian church.

I want to introduce myself a little bit so you will know who I am. I have been a Christian since 1985. I left Iran as a teenager and met the gospel in a Christian community through the ministry of some American missionaries in Europe. I submitted to the Lordship of Christ as a 16-year-old Iranian Muslim teenager and have been on this journey walking with Christ ever since. I now teach and equip Iranian churches.

I have been involved with Iranian Christians outside of Iran since 1988; for the past 22 years, I have been deeply involved with the Christian community in Iran and with the diaspora. I've had the privilege of being a teacher in the Iranian Christian world for the past two decades. I have connected deeply with the official building (brick and mortar) churches inside Iran, the house church movement in Iran, and the Iranian churches and fellowships worldwide. I have taught at conferences and seminars and have presented on satellite TV. Through the work of Pars Theological Centre, I'm involved in teaching and training a generation of new Iranian leaders.

The topic of abusive and toxic leadership in the church has been a very important theme in my own teaching over the past two decades. I am very pleased that we are addressing this subject head-on and not shying away from some of the very difficult conversations we need to have in the church.

I thought that the best way for me to speak on this topic is to take you along with me on my journey for the past 20 years as a kind of autobiographical overview of how I came into this conversation. You will notice three stages in my own development as I walk you through my journey.

The first time that I became aware of toxic leadership was in 1999 at a conference. I met Iranian Christians who lived in Iran when they came out for a short period of time for training and then they would go back inside the country. I was a translator for a very well-known Armenian/Lebanese speaker who had come to speak to our Iranian group. He made a comment that deeply impacted my life, ministry, and teaching. He said, "In my 30 years of ministry in the Middle East, I have never seen a pastor confess to a sin or admit to a mistake and ask for forgiveness." That shocked me. I know the state of the church in the Middle East and the kind of problems that we are facing with the issues of pride and ego of many Christian leaders. But to hear that kind of admission from a prominent and respected leader was astonishing. Maybe our own people put leaders on a spiritual pedestal as if pastors never struggle with anything, never make any mistakes, never have any struggles with sin in their lives and, somehow, are on a different spiritual level. When I heard that, I said that I want to be the kind of Iranian leader and model for the Iranian community that breaks that mould. I want to go against that trend of hiding behind a title or a position. I want to make myself vulnerable and talk about my struggles, sins, and mistakes. It was at that time I decided to put a lot of focus on presenting and introducing authors and writings that I thought would be helpful in addressing this issue. For those who know me and my style of teaching, I am passionate about introducing good Christian authors and good books to the Iranian church. Some of these books have Farsi translations and have deeply impacted other Iranian believers and leaders. My special calling and ministry are to be a bridge introducing wonderful resources from the churches in the West to the church in Iran.

For example, I sent Henri Nouwen's *In the Name of Jesus: Reflections on Christian Leadership* and Brennan Manning's *Abba's Child: The Cry of the Heart for Intimate Belonging* to Iran which were translated into Farsi. I started presenting these authors who talk about vulnerability, authenticity, and brokenness. The image I presented was that even Christian leaders are broken. We are wounded healers ourselves. We are called into positions of leadership but that doesn't mean that we are perfect without any struggles in our lives. We can have deep struggles and yet be faithful in following Jesus and being leaders in the church. That was the first stage of my development as it relates to the issues of abuse and toxic leadership. In this stage, I emphasised the theme of vulnerability and brokenness through the writings of Henri Nouwen and Brennan Manning. This included the theme of grace to make ourselves and our vulnerabilities known, while being anchored in the grace of God. Books like Phil Yancey's *The Jesus I Never Knew* and Larry Crab's *Inside Out* are further examples of authors talking about the vulnerabilities of leaders. These authors and themes help us to become real with who we are with our own struggles while hanging on to God's grace and reflecting that grace in our relationship with others in the church. That was my first stage in this conversation and the emphasis in my teaching. I was presenting a positive impression of the ideal church leader.

The second stage in my development of understanding toxic leadership came a few years later. Like before, it was precipitated by a conversation at a conference which impacted me significantly. This time, I was in Berlin and teaching through Phil Yancey's book, *The Jesus I Never Knew*. On the second day of the conference, an Iranian man from somewhere in Europe pulled me aside and asked if he could talk to me. I said, "sure". His very first question was this, "Aren't you ashamed of yourself?" I was surprised, but smiled and said, "No, why?" "You have all these beautiful teachings and themes inviting us to enter God's grace and you trick people to enter Iranian churches. When we enter these churches, we encounter all kinds of abuses and authoritarian leadership." He gave me examples of what he and others have experienced in some churches. I honestly don't know if they were all true, or exaggerated, or if it was his perspective or experiences.

I was absolutely shocked to hear some of these stories. For example, a pastor would do a favour for a refugee in Europe and help them settle into a new home. Because he did this to help them, now the refugees needed to obey the pastor, attend church, and submit to the pastor. The pastor's perspective was, since he had done this favour for them, they now owed the pastor their obedience. If the refugee refused to obey the pastor, he would report the family to the authorities to deport them back to Iran. I was so shocked by those stories I was hearing. I told this gentleman that the only thing I can do is to bring some teachings to address this topic.

I came back to the United States and found Stephen Arterburn's *Toxic Faith: Experiencing Healing from Painful Spiritual Abuse*. I presented that book on satellite TV and received some pushback from some Iranian pastors in Iran who said, "You are bringing shame to the church by talking about these problems. All the Iranian mullahs are so toxic and corrupt. Why are you highlighting the problems of a toxic church?" I remember the week I was recording this program in a studio in Nashville, TN, the American media was focused on abuse in the Catholic church. I kept on saying that this isn't a Catholic or Protestant problem, nor a Christian or Muslim problem, for any system can become toxic. It can be a religious system, an organisation, a family, or a government that becomes toxic. Stephen Arterburn, after he wrote *Toxic Faith*, wrote another book, *More Jesus, Less Religion: Moving from Rules to Relationship*. I entitled that series, *The Characteristics of a Healthy Faith*. I have taught that many times in conferences and seminars. I have received a lot of positive feedback. The second stage of my emphasis in teaching was on toxicity, abuse, authoritarianism, manipulation, fear, legalism, black and white thinking, with us or against us mentality, and issues of control.

The third stage in my development of understanding toxic leadership came a few years later. I was encountering a lot of burnout among Iranian believers and church leaders because of an unhealthy approach to ministry and life. I started reading the writings of Peter Scazzero, such as *Emotionally Healthy Church, Updated and Expanded Edition; Emotionally Healthy Spirituality: It's Impossible to Be Spiritually Mature; While Remaining Emotionally Immature;* and *The Emotionally Healthy Leader: How Transforming Your Inner Life Will Deeply Transform Your Church, Team, and the World.* His *Emotionally Healthy Church* has been a major focus of my third stage in the development of this theme. I taught the meaning of a healthy church, a healthy Christian life, and a healthy style of leadership. Peter Scazzero highlights setting limits, grieving well, and living in vulnerability and brokenness. I keep emphasising these themes. I have seen how Iranian leaders and believers respond very positively to these themes. In addition, I taught that we need to be safe people. Henry Cloud and John Townsend's *Safe People: How to Find Relationships That Are Good for You and Avoid Those That Aren't* and *Boundaries Face to Face: How To Have That Difficult Conversation You've Been Avoiding* became key texts which I taught. In this stage, I focused on how to move to become a safe church, a safe friend, and a safe leader. To do that, we need to respect boundaries, our own and others' boundaries. We have seen phenomenally positive feedback on this type of teaching through Pars Theological Centre's conferences and testimonies from our students. There is a lot of misinformation and misunderstanding regarding the ministry. Ministry is plagued by a lack of boundaries, safety, and a healthy approach to life and leadership in Iranian Christian circles.

Good teaching may not result in good outcomes every time. I remember the very first time that I taught at a seminar with Dr Mehrdad Fatehi at the very first Pars seminar with a wonderful network of Iranian Christian leaders from Iran. I taught through *Emotionally Healthy Church* and the book *Safe People*. Those Iranian leaders went back to Iran. About two years later, I saw some of those leaders and they all talked about how much of an impact those books and my teaching had made on their life, faith, and ministry. To my dismay, because of that teaching, the church network split up. The reason for the split was that they had realised just how toxic and manipulative their key leaders were. I didn't know if I should be happy that they felt so transformed or if I should be sad that this teaching caused a split of a significant church network. I'm still thinking about that issue.

So often the abusive toxic style of leadership is hidden, and people don't talk about it because of shame or fear. Here are some of the stories I heard: One leader would tell another leader under his supervision that he should not have any children because there are so many ministry needs that it's selfish to have children. His advice to the pastor was to devote himself wholly to the work of the Lord. Another scenario was to tell new pastors that they cannot study what they desire in the university because there are a lot of ministry needs. They were to devote themselves to evangelism and not pursue another career or field of study. This type of control and manipulation has been my third stage of learning about toxic and abusive leadership. I emphasise emotional health, safety, and boundaries. I encouraged people to respect everyone's distinctive calling, makeup, and the unique way people grow spiritually and relate to God. I emphasised individual freedom for each person to relate to God and the way the Spirit of God is leading and shaping them. The tendency in the Iranian church is to have the leader be totally in charge. The leader makes the decision on what they are to do, controls others' lives in minute detail, and is the anointed one who seems to have a special relationship with God. Therefore, the attendee must check all their decisions and get the approval of the leader for every decision that they want to make in life. The leader makes all the judgments, and they must make sure to appease the leader. These are very unhealthy trends in the Iranian world throughout our history and culture that translate to a lot of toxicity and abuse within the Iranian church.

I don't have just one solution for what we are facing, but what I have been doing for the past 20-plus years is to keep teaching about relevant books and authors. I want to keep modelling the kind of authenticity, vulnerability, grace, safety, boundaries, and a healthy style of life and faith I want others to see. We need to keep teaching, modelling, relating, and challenging the classical paradigm that the leader knows everything, and all must submit to the leader.

These are the three stages of my journey in how I interact with the themes of toxicity and abuse of the authoritarian structure in the Iranian context. We have so many stories of a pastor getting upset and expelling people from the church. If any member offends the pastor for any reason, such as the pastor's insecurity, lack of knowledge, or experience, whenever the pastor feels threatened or challenged, he feels free to expel people from the church and accuse them of rebellion and sin. This kind of authoritarian approach to ministry through control and manipulation creates a culture of fear. The lack of transparency must be addressed. Under this type of leadership, people cannot be honest about their life and must pretend that they are perfect. I teach against that kind of paradigm. I keep introducing authors that bring a sense of freedom, being real, and living in God's grace.

I want to close by telling our Western friends that this is not just an Iranian or Middle Eastern problem, or even a Muslim problem. This is just a common human nature problem. A recent book could be a new stage in my journey on dealing with this topic. The new book is Scott McKnight's *A Church Called TOV: Forming a Goodness Culture That Resists Abuses of Power and Promotes Healing*. Scott McKnight talks about the abuse in the American church and the fall of some of the very prominent pastors, Christian leaders, and leaders of Christian parachurch organisations. We see the same kind of toxicity and abuse in many American churches and ministries as we experience in the Middle East. There is the fear factor, the isolation of the leader from the community, and the sense that the leader is not accountable and not transparent to anybody. McKnight gives us some direction: we must nurture empathy and resist a narcissist culture; nurture grace and resist a fear culture; nurture justice and resist a loyalty culture; nurture service and resist a celebrity culture of leadership; and nurture a Christlikeness and resist a leader culture. McKnight talks about the American church, but these themes speak directly to the Iranian context. My hope is that, by emphasising the antidote to toxicity and abusive leadership, we can gradually see the Iranian church moving toward becoming a safe place. We want to see safe, humble, Christlike servant leaders who are nurturing the church in goodness, in *tov* (Hebrew for "good"), in a Christlike example.

Discussions on Abusive and Toxic Leadership

The following is drawn from discussions conducted in breakout rooms followed by the panel discussion. Some of the material has been translated from the original Farsi. The focus in this section are Iranians, except where stated otherwise. Several of the contributors note the applicability to other ethnicities. Each subsection is derived from one contributor and the many subsections are drawn from several speakers.

The Role of Western Churches and Agencies: Mature Western churches, leaders, and agencies have an important role to play in moving the BMB churches toward good health. They need to come alongside the emerging leadership of the BMB church. Of course, not all Western leaders and agencies are a picture of good health. The emerging church is looking for humble, vulnerable, authentic, and healthy mission agencies to assist them. It is important to develop those friendships and role models in mature Western Christian churches to help the BMB church move towards a healthier version. For example, I've texted a friend asking if his mission agency could become more engaged with the Iranian world. His response was that the Iranian church is doing fine on its own and doesn't need help. He asked if that is an accurate picture. I responded, not quite. We don't need evangelists to come, but we could use good coaches, elder brothers and sisters who walk this journey of faith with us to mentor, encourage, and teach us. A lot of the problems happen because church leaders work in isolation. I see an equal amount of dysfunction in the Western church, so I don't blame Islam alone for our situation. Role models and friends are very important to walk with us on this journey, in addition to good teaching and books.

Origin of Toxic Leaders: Can we say those leaders from a Muslim-background struggle with toxic leadership because, in Islam, the nature of God is to only love those who love him? Is it because the Islamic God is mostly a voluntarist God?[10]

Yes, Islamic theology brings with it its own problems about toxic leadership. As a patriarchal society, Iranian culture is different than American society, and American history is radically different than Iranian history. What makes it even more complex is that, within the country, there are different local expressions of the problem. But in our mission circles, there is too much blame put on Islam or Iran and I see the same mess in American churches. Someone asked me the question, "How in the world is the Iranian church growing with all these problems?" My answer is that Willow Creek Church in the Chicago area didn't have a Muslim problem and it was a growing, flourishing church, yet it had a deeply toxic and dysfunctional leadership. Scott McKnight discusses this very problem in his book, *A Church Called TOV*. Behind the facade of Willow Creek Church was a wonderful visionary leader and all the wonderful programmes, but he was an isolated leader who controlled people, and people were afraid to confront him.

When Should Teaching Leadership Begin? When we talk about leadership, the paradigm under which we are working is to have students come to a seminary. There, we train them to become leaders, but this is too late. Discipleship is one of the answers to our problem with toxic leadership. We need a comprehensive view of leadership that starts with discipleship from the very beginning of one's Christian life. From the moment that someone comes to church, discipleship needs to lay the foundation for leadership. From the very beginning, we need to teach humility and self-sacrifice. We need to teach and model leadership humility as seen in Philippians 2:3-4. Brick by brick, we need to build mature disciples in the church. Another aspect is to talk about the problems of leadership, so that the new disciple becomes self-aware of the problem of toxic leadership. This will give us a point of reference to address the problem. However, in the Iranian culture, it is assumed that if we talk about something, it will be resolved.

For example, in Iran people constantly talk about corruption. Yet, Iran is one of the most corrupt countries in the world. Iranian leaders talk about corruption, but no one does anything about the problem. This can happen in the church as well. Because we talk about toxic and authoritarian leadership, our practice is to continue with the current form of leadership in our churches. We deceive ourselves by saying that we know the problem exists and we have talked about

---

[10] Voluntarism is a *meta-ethical* doctrine according to which actions are right in virtue of God's willing them. "Voluntarism", *New World Encyclopedia*, [Available at: https://www.newworldencyclopedia.org/entry/Voluntarism], [Last accessed: 28th September 2024].

it, so the problem has been addressed. Talking about the problems is good, but just talking about them doesn't mean we are solving them.

One trend in independent or mega-churches is to become their own missionary sending agencies. They do their own recognisance, put together a short-term team, and do their own training, but the team often has not studied the culture beyond a surface understanding. They then meet with a national leader, who culturally presents himself as a leader of a large network of house churches. The Western team gets excited about supporting what appears to be a good national leader, believing the message without verification. Perhaps they are just enabling a toxic leader.

Another trend in missions is the view that Westerners coming in too strong with our Western theology or culture would destroy the indigenous movement taking place. On the national church front, the national worker at times views the Western church as a source of income, so they do their best to present a very positive, healthy, and growing movement which they are leading. The Western team has no context to doubt what is presented to them and they support the leader with everything he/she asks for. We need to determine in what way the Western church should come in and help.

Developing Counsellors to Help with Toxic Leadership: There is no easy solution. I love the idea that leadership starts with discipleship. One thing that I have been contemplating is that our focus on discipleship places too much emphasis on experts and how it undermines the priesthood of all believers. We have elevated the leader or expert to do all the work for us, and then we have someone to blame when something goes wrong. That is very selfish of us. We desire to have a hero to save us from all our problems, yet we are not willing to step up and take the risks ourselves. We need to tell the leaders that if they want to be healthy leaders, they must have counsel around them like David had Nathan counsel him. They need more than just one Nathan to help guide the leader to nurture the DNA of servant leadership. We need to talk about it often so no leader can say, "I don't need others around to counsel me."

Isn't the situation that most of these churches that we are talking about are house churches, where there are no Nathans or Jonathans to help? In a Western setting, there are a lot of mature healthy people who can give godly counsel, but in the emerging church, there are not a lot of mature Christians to draw upon.

The Bible admonishes us to have many advisers and not to keep our own counsel. This is where leaders in isolation keep their own counsel. It needs to be shouted from the rooftops how sinful the current phenomenon of leaders working alone is. There is no good that can come out of that in the long run. If you want churches and ministries to multiply and thrive under your leadership, they can't keep their own counsel.

I was wondering about the concept of Nathans. You who work among Iranian congregations, do you have experience with how these Nathans are developed? For example, how do you encourage new believers to become Nathans in the discipleship process? Is there a structure for this? When we think about the priesthood of all believers, the Nathans don't have to be very special people, so everyone should become a type of Nathan.

In the Chicago area, there have been eight Iranian churches that started and all eight of them have failed. In the most recent one, I tried to become a Nathan and it worked for a while until the leader "received a divine calling from God" to go somewhere else. This left the church in an absolute mess. I worked with a young emerging leader to keep the fellowship going. Then the leader who left had another "divine calling from God" to return to the Chicago area six months later. He asked everyone in the former fellowship to repent, since in his opinion, they had spoken ill of him. He portrayed himself as God's gift to reach Iranians in the Chicago area. He said he would start a new fellowship, but not steal people from the struggling fellowship. But soon afterwards, he did contact all the others in the struggling fellowship and invited them to his new church. He found an independent charismatic church that welcomed him to use their facility to start his new fellowship. This only created more confusion and a greater split in the Iranian Christian community. We can have Nathans come alongside, but one problem is when the toxic leader believes that God speaks directly to him and he should only listen to the Holy Spirit for guidance. He believes he has a direct connection with God, but not with any counsellors or advisors.

Nathan had two roles with David. One was to support David and the other was to confront him. Iranian pastors like the supportive Nathans, someone just to be helpful and to encourage them. It is very difficult for the Iranian leadership to listen to criticism from anyone. Currently, Iranian churches are not ready for this type of mentoring, which includes corrective criticism. In our culture, it is not permissible to criticise someone in charge. The Iranian leadership model of authoritarianism is dominant. We like someone to be supportive like Nathan, but not confront us. Typically, this second side of Nathan does not happen in our culture or within the church culture. Therefore, we need to change our paradigm about leadership to accept both support and correction.

I have been thinking about how we can come up with a plan to help the new Muslim-background churches. From a practical point of view, it is difficult to find good leaders that are mature enough to lead a Christian group, with an awareness of how to lead without creating/maintaining a toxic atmosphere. It is very difficult for us to find someone like this in our Christian community in the Middle East. It is so much harder to find someone in a new church or fellowship coming from a Muslim background. We cannot wait until we find a good leader to start a church because the people need a church or fellowship and a leader to lead the fellowship. We need some practical steps to address the immediate need for small churches and I trust that this resource assists many.

The other issue is the expectation of the congregation of that small church. Sadly, people coming from Middle Eastern cultural backgrounds are looking for a leader to tell them what to do and to blindly follow him/her. They will not grow in their faith and mature with this type of leadership. Without it, the people will feel that they don't even have a leader. How can we help them to balance the various expectations the people bring with them? How can we help leaders balance the biblical model of leadership and, at the same time, not lose the trust of the people with the expectation of what the culture says is a mark of a good leader? I really would like to see some practical steps on what to do.

The Complexities of Strong Leaders – Congregations' Expectations: Our first contributor, in her talk on communication, explained that Iranians are looking for a hero to come in and lead the people. The leader is to have a strong personality and the members are to submit to the person with absolute loyalty. This then feeds the cultural expectations. There is a role to be played on the leadership side and on the congregational side in responding to biblical leadership.

Two things come to mind. First is the expectation of others doing something that you are not doing yourself. This doesn't give a very strong message. If I am the pastor or leader, I need to openly demonstrate that I have counsellors that I work with. Second, why do we have so many toxic leaders? Perhaps because that is what the congregation wants. They want a leader to tell them what to do and not have to think about it. I have been in a discipleship relationship in which we met as peers. We would study the Bible together as peers, yet someone in this study said that this type of study is a lot more difficult. It is much easier to talk with another person who just tells me what to do. These two approaches need to be balanced together.

The last comment is about having trust and modelling humility, and yet the church expects an authoritarian leader. These leaders act like sheiks, who have confidence that they know more than those in the fellowship, and they have God's divine knowledge as their shepherds of what the people are to do in their lives. It is a balancing act for leaders living in a shame and honour collective culture. They need to maintain the authority and honour that is needed to be a good leader in that culture, and yet model humility in ways that are appropriate.

As a Westerner serving in the context of the Iranian church for over 40 years, I realised that I had to work within the system of the culture and the worldview. I could be a benevolent and loving non-toxic leader. The churches that I pastored wanted me to be an authoritative and strong leader. The first criticism I received was that I was too weak as a leader and that I was too open to everybody's ideas. So I met with my leaders on an individual basis to find out where their hearts really were and began to model with them what it means to be a servant leader. You can't go against the system; you must work within it. For example, you can't change the language, you have to learn the language. But you can be a godly example. I spend much of my time visiting and spending personal time with Iranian pastors, living in their homes, and talking with their wives. Toxic leadership affects marriages and women are being badly abused in some of these homes. It is important for those of us who understand these principles to fully practice them. We have to do it within the context of the culture and model it in a way that shows that an authoritative leader doesn't have to be toxic, but be servant-oriented and a blessing to others.

The Complexity of Strong Leaders: Being directive as a strong leader is only one of many strategies for making decisions. If being directive is the default, then that is not healthy.

Authority in the shame/honour culture is to be directive. That is what is expected. In the collective culture, controlling authority is a standard part of being a valued, honoured leader.

Definitely, the culture needs to be addressed. The whole process takes time, and the new church doesn't have it. We need to come up with an immediate solution for how we can help the new church coming from a Muslim background in the Middle East. Creating a church for this new group coming from a Muslim background has a lot of challenges. We need time to create healthy leaders, yet the BMBs need a church right now. How can we help the church to go through the process, so both the leader and the congregation can mature and learn how the church should be?

Example of Developing Good Leaders: At Pars Theological Centre, as we are training leaders all over the Iranian world, we seek to have structures where young emerging leaders are in a community of learning with other young emerging leaders. No one expects the young evangelist church planter to have the maturity of our teachers, but to encourage that learning is a lifelong process. We have had many people in the Middle East, Arab and Persian, who after they graduated from seminary rarely read another book. They thought that they had finished their learning. Being in a community of life-long learners, being in a network of other church planters and leaders learning from each other, means being mentored and directed by older and more mature leaders. This would be a very practical step we can do – and model – for the younger generation.

An African proverb that has become popular in America is, "It takes a village to raise a child." It is not just the parents who are needed to raise a child, but a whole village. Applying this principle to the church, "It takes the whole church to raise leaders." We have talked about the role of Western churches, but we have limited resources. At Pars, we do our best to produce books and courses, translating books on leadership, but at the same time, we need the cooperation of the churches. This process will take one or two generations. It is a misnomer to think that after ten years we will have wonderful mature leaders. The awareness and seriousness of the problems the nascent church faces is a great place to start. But the church needs years and years of teaching. Discipleship needs to be redefined in creating a good environment for future leaders. In the long term, we will have good leaders, but we will still have bad and toxic leaders.

Qualifications of Good Leaders: Can we look for a person who has the character of a leader, if not the skills of a leader? Character is much more important than skill. I think about Moses in Numbers 12:3: "Now Moses was a very humble man, more humble than anyone else on the face of the earth." I think humility is what people are looking for, which is strength under control. Leadership teams may work in some churches, if they work together to help each other grow and mature in leadership. In the Arab world, there are leadership teams that sometimes work. We should try many things to address this need.

I like the idea of a leadership team. It has its own issues, but toxic leadership doesn't thrive as well on a team. But there are other problems that thrive on leadership teams.

Modelling Learning: Is it easy for your professors at Pars to model that they are still learners, or are they the knowledgeable experts that are teaching rather than modelling learning?

That is one thing we model very well at Pars.

That is crucial. In living in a collective culture of honour, the expectation is that the leader or teacher knows everything, and the teacher is going to impart this knowledge through rote learning and teach it to their students.

At Pars, we have many weaknesses, but on the topic of developing a culture of learning, we have modelled it well. They are always seeing us reading books, studying, and referring to authors. For example, Dr Fatehi has his Ph.D. in New Testament; when he was doing a course on the Trinity, he read the latest books and did months of new research. The students are always seeing the faculty develop fresh research projects. We are creating a culture of learning.

Should We Be Concerned About Too Much Influence from the West? There is a trend in missions that includes the Discipleship Making Movement (DMM), in which the leaders of DMM don't want any Western influence. They feel that the best theology should come out of the indigenous culture without influencing how to do church. There is a strong influence, particularly in the West, of this type of model for church multiplication. Is the hands-off approach the best way to avoid these problems?

From personal experience, I did not experience any resistance from the local congregation that feels that Western white American's or white European's influence is not desired. You might get that kind of resistance from the local leaders, but not from the church itself. If I were one of the leaders of the Western organisations or churches, and I really feel that God is leading us to do something in this area of the world, I should be open to learning about the local culture, but not be scared of negatively influencing the culture. The local congregation really wants to hear from the Western missionary. The Arab church seems to be more open to hearing something that has a different perspective than what they have been hearing thus far. They prefer to hear someone from outside their culture than someone from within their own culture. There is resistance when Westerners come with zero knowledge of anything Middle Eastern with their training manuals with the expectation that the local leader follows it. But if Western organisations come with a humble attitude, being led by the Holy Spirit, they can be very helpful.

How to Deal with Toxic Leaders: In the DMM, the healthiest expressions are in the later stage of maturity. This is when there is a great emphasis on healthy partnerships. Sometimes unhealthy partnerships are caused when the local leaders will feel threatened. The other side is when the outside influencers try to exert more influence than is warranted. It undermines the healthy growing fellowship. But when it is healthy, there is a welcoming of counsel. These healthy fellowships act like the Bereans in Acts 17, by checking with the scriptures to see if what was taught is true. They try to understand how God is leading and are open to considering if there is something that needs to be changed or learned. The healthy Discipleship Making Movements have very healthy partnerships with outside influencers. The outside influencers are not trying to overly influence, but want to support and strengthen the local leaders.

It may be helpful as translated Western books are read by the congregation or the pastor, to help them understand that a certain point works in their context but needs to be tweaked in our context.

Show People that They Are Important: I think that people prefer being with others who are not acting, but are being themselves. They can easily differentiate between these two. People are intuitive and know when someone is showing their true self or hiding their true self. This usually happens out of the fear of their problems being revealed.

We also need to show people that they are important to us. It means spending time with them and listening to them. Many Iranian Christians feel that no one is listening to them or cares about them. We should feel their pain – just as Jesus felt people's pain.

Culturally, we Iranians don't show what is in our hearts. We, as leaders, really love people but we don't show that love to them.

Confession of a Toxic Leader: I was both a toxic leader, as well as having worked with the toxic leaders who mentored me. Unfortunately, most of my service was in the area where I was toxic and poisoned others. We should be transparent in our conversations. We should express the weaknesses that we have, announce them, and become friends with church members.

I am in the process of maturing and God is still working on me. Spending time with people is important and we need to talk about our rough edges with them. Our openness to everyone helps people to trust us and we should even allow them to criticise us. We must have the humility to accept that this is counter-cultural for those of us from the Middle East.

Doing the Right Thing: I remember a story. A teacher came to the class and said to his students, "Do what I say, don't do what I do." It seems that we do the same in the church when we don't have the right model. But thank God that we realise that what we do is wrong, and we want to do the right thing.

Iranian Churches Have Both Toxic Leaders and Toxic Members: Members in the Iranian church are mostly new believers, and they look to the leaders as their examples. So, when the leaders become more like Christ, the members become like Christ too. But when preachers don't grow, unfortunately, this creates a gap between preachers and leaders. Sometimes it is good for leaders to seek prayers for themselves. This will help people to realise that we are human just like them.

People in the church should understand that leaders are weak, we sin, we cry, and we get sad and depressed. We are humans too. When we look at the Bible, we find that not everyone was a great or perfect person. The men of God are generally weak, for example, David and Moses. Yet when we humble ourselves, God will exalt us.

As leaders of the Church of Iran, we need to humble ourselves in front of the members and not be afraid of how people look at us.

We should not be swayed by people's applause, curses, or the stones they throw at us. The goal is to be faithful servants of the people with God's help and live as God wants us to live. Let's talk about our pains, weaknesses, and problems, and we can grow together in that way.

Get to the Root of the Problem: What is the root of toxic problems and why does a leader become toxic? In my opinion, toxic leaders are insecure and sway towards a controlling model because they feel that they have no control over the situation. They may also believe that members are better than they are, or they have more knowledge, or they have better leadership skills than the leader.

I'll use an analogy to illustrate my point. There is a leadership chair that everyone wants to grab and sit on. The toxic leader believes that he/she/they are firmly attached to this seat. Whoever wants to take the leadership chair from the leader will hit them in the head and tell them to move aside so that another leader can have this place of authority.

Now, what are the privileges of such a leader sticking to that chair? It is either they are getting good money from the churches, or they are looking for the prestige and fame that the church gives.

People who are placed into leadership positions are often not psychologically ready for this position. They may have studied theology and may have some leadership skills. But has this person been healed from inside wounds? Something has made them insecure. What experiences did they have in the past that have led them to a leadership control model?

Before we choose a leader, it is necessary to think about the mental health of our leaders. Jesus Christ can heal these wounds. But the reality is that, besides God's intervention, we must also provide a series of psychological interventions for our leaders and make leaders' mental health a priority. Maybe we need to send him to a Christian psychologist to get help or have them go to psychological therapy sessions.

Many of these problems can be rooted in their childhood and we forget this part. Let's invest in the mental health of our leaders and then reap the rewards in the future. Then, we will have better churches and the members will be happier.

Second, we have the wrong understanding of leadership. Leadership means that I bend down and give a chance to the next person to step his foot on my back and move up to a higher position. The current Iranian understanding of leadership puts them in control, while others are running behind them. But leadership is not like that. We confuse management and being a boss with being a leader. The true leader is someone who says, "Sir, put your foot on my back and go two steps higher, and I will be happy if you go ahead of me in this."

I am researching and interviewing people about what is happening in the Iranian churches in Turkey. The problem can be traced to the main leader who worked with several other leaders under him. The other leaders never allowed people or members to visit or call that main leader, say hello to him, or establish a relationship with him. They were told that they should always deal with these secondary leaders in the local church.

What does this indicate? It means that the structures in place are defective. Maybe the institution that was providing services to these people thought that members were crossing their boundaries. But the boundaries were not democratically chosen.

Boundaries: I am currently writing a book in which I talk about the idea that boundaries should be chosen in a collaborative way. We should not decide our own boundaries and tell the members that they should conform to these rules. Members should be happy too. We need to ask the members whether they will benefit from my boundary settings and whether they will observe them or not.

Another thing that is happening in the Iranian church is that the shepherd or the leader sets boundaries based on his own framework and does not involve the members. In fact, people and members are not happy or satisfied with what is happening. It expresses itself in the fact that the members have no right to talk to others. These boundaries are toxic and unhealthy. So, we must work on the leader's insecurities and teach the qualities of a good leader. They are to have good characteristics, be flexible, choose collaboratively, and choose wisely based on the needs and conditions of the group.

Talking about Leadership and Toxicity: Training future leaders should be intentional. We should educate a new generation of leaders with good teaching and setting good examples. A lot of work needs to be done to change the future, for people look to their leaders as examples. I have personally experienced toxic behaviour and I've heard my friends talk about it. I spoke against toxic behaviour when their role models and leaders were behaving in a toxic manner. After several years of seeing these leaders in different situations, I was surprised. These leaders have not changed, for they continue with the same toxic leadership model.

Education of the next generation is very important, and we should talk about this issue. We must teach a new culture of leadership regularly in our lessons, on television, in leadership training, and in servant-building courses. It should be talked about so much that it is recognised as a positive model. This is healthy leadership. And conversely, that type of toxic leadership should be talked about as creating negative role models everywhere. This will create at least some self-awareness.

The next point is that we really need to encourage leaders to have mentors. As it was said, Pars Theological Center has started a counselling centre to help our future leaders. I believe that many of our leaders need counselling. It will take more than one or two counselling sessions for they need inner healing to change those wounds that are old and lingering.

IQ, BQ, and EQ: Your words hit the right spot. This is what we need, inner healing to change those wounds that are old and lingering. The pains and problems that exist in Turkey are also present in Europe and America respectively, but with less intensity. It depends on how long we have been in those countries and how we grew up. We grew up with leaders and servants for several years and learned a series of issues. As someone said, "Let's go to the solution." The solution is for me to change. We all need to change.

I am sure you have all heard about IQ tests. For example, say that a person's IQ is high. Then we come to Christianity – instead of IQ, I use the word BQ (for Bible intelligence). It means your Bible Q is high. We get BQ when we go to college and learn Christian clichés. Then, I go to the pulpit. Yes, my BQ is high, but there is another word that is used a lot in America, which is EQ. It means emotional intelligence. This is the capacity to be aware of, control, and express one's emotions and to handle interpersonal relationships rightly and with empathy. In other words, I don't get angry easily, depressed, or frustrated. Thus, I named these IQ, BQ, and EQ.

One person comes into the church with a high BQ. Naturally, his IQ is obviously high too, but unfortunately, this is not the case with the balance of his EQ. This person becomes one of the worst servants and damages the church, particularly if he has been abused since childhood. When he is asked to be the pastor of the church, that person will damage the church members. That is why we need to change ourselves.

I know a Christian who came from Iran and has been a servant for 42 years; he has come through all these pains. It is an honour for me to see how much he has been healed, and now he serves in our church. I also needed a lot of healing myself. I did so much damage to others and to the church. I have been a pastor for 21 years; I hurt people during my pastorate. Now, I teach a series of healing and freedom lessons that I learned myself.

EQ is the most important issue here. All Muslim-born people, including me, need spiritual warfare. If we are not aware of how to deal with spiritual warfare issues, we will be beaten in the battle. Evil spirits and Islam control and manipulate us. Thus, the spirit of control, the spirit of death, and the spirit of fear enter the church.

So, servants like me and us, are identified by the service we have while we are in conflict with three issues: position, possession (office), and ownership. These three things must go and be replaced by mission, responsibility, and commitment.

We, as leaders, are stuck. A future leader sits in our church and observes how he should behave in the pulpit. He then senses God's anointing and studies the Bible. When he comes to our churches, his BQ is high and we enjoy how he interprets the Bible for us. Yet, he goes home and fights with his wife. And this is the leader of the church. Someone should at least ask him, "Where is your priority?" As someone said, "There are a bunch of us who are dysfunctional, with damaged lives and when we come to leadership, we get angry and abuse people." We need repentance. We are in a spiritual battle. We need freedom. The good news is this problem can be solved. I have seen this and thank God for this. We now have a healing and freedom clinic that is for shepherds. I now have at least 30 pastors and I am working with them. I am rarely surprised by what I hear, for I have had many problems myself. This clinic is not only for the people of Iran, but also for pastors. It is a place where we can talk about these issues.

Small Groups: I am learning from all of you dear ones. I have thought about this issue a lot. I have been looking for a leadership model for the Iranian church for years. In addition to the things that the dear leaders said before, such as healing and mentoring, which are all very important, we need to form small groups of leaders at different levels. These leaders should have a healing space there to participate in and talk about these issues together and for all of us to come together and talk about the issues which have happened in our churches. Leaders need to open themselves up and help each other. I taught Iranian students for 10 years. They can learn a principle, but they could not apply it. There is a deep valley between head knowledge and heart knowledge in our people.

The way to fill this void, in addition to having a coach or mentors, we need a space like this where we gather together and learned to be vulnerable. Let's talk about family matters. We shouldn't use terms like "we leaders" and "them". Instead, we say that we have these issues and problems. We should talk about our personal problems, such as a problem with my wife, a problem with my daughter, and a problem with my pastor. How do we deal with these issues? Let's pray for each other. Let's not judge each other. I think that this could be a healing space which is very important for us to sit down and talk about these issues.

I have coached and mentored for many years. I feel that this issue is missing. People, especially Iranian leaders, should talk about their challenges and concerns, which are many. Whenever we talk about leadership in Iran, we consider the "trait model" – that is, a leader who has good characteristics. So, all the leaders who are in these meetings think that they should be good Christian leaders. Our starting point has always been the "trait model", which causes people to come and say that we are good. We avoid talking about challenges because we don't know how to implement them in our own lives or for others. Why? Because we lack modelling. I think this is missing in our leadership models.

Spiritual Warfare: We Iranians come from different traditions, such as Evangelical and Pentecostal. We have different views and thank God for this diversity. But there is a taboo or fear of talking about spiritual warfare. We must face it. Islam's effects are evident in our churches. But we rarely deal with them. As one person said, we need to change.

The leader/pastor knows all his theological positions. He wants to change, but there are demonic forces influencing him. We must recognise these evil forces. I am not saying that we should go to extremes. The pastor can have problems he carries since childhood, such as his father humiliating him. There are physical abuses in Iran of both boys and girls. These abuses must be resolved before the pastor is given the role of the shepherd of the church. Yes, we must heal within through counselling but also fight the evil forces on the outside. The servant must know these two dimensions. If both realities are not addressed, if when the shepherd enters the pastorate and both realities are not addressed, his authority will be hindered.

Conclusion

The first thing presented was the role of mature Western churches, leaders, and agencies when it comes to addressing the problem of toxic leaders. The emerging BMB churches and the Christian background churches need help in navigating the cultural complexities of leadership in North African, Middle Eastern, and Iranian contexts. Several discussions addressed the problems that happen because the leader works in isolation.

A question was raised if Islamic theology leads to toxic leadership. It was recognised that Islamic theology does have its own problems, but Western culture also has problems with toxic leadership. However, each culture has its own unique expressions. It was suggested that the phenomenon of toxic leadership needs to be addressed when a person comes to Christ, not when they become leaders. The cultural expectation of leadership should start in the discipleship process from the very beginning of the Christian life for both the leaders and followers. They both need a proper understanding of biblical leadership. By raising the issue at the start of a Christian life, new believers will become self-aware of the problem of toxic leadership and the role they all play in it.

The complexities of toxic leadership come in various forms. First, believers desire to have a hero to save them from all their problems. Second, it was recognised that leaders should not work in isolation. Yet the context of most emerging churches is that there is a dearth of leaders, so someone with natural abilities automatically seizes or is pushed into leadership as a young immature Christian. Third, the values of the culture desire the leader to tell the members what to do and think, and the congregation expects the leader to take on this role. This sets up a pattern that leads to toxic leadership. Fourth, people look for those who have skills in leadership. It was suggested we need to look for a person who has the character of a leader, not the skills of a leader. Character is much more important than the skills of a leader. Practically speaking, it was suggested that it may take one or two generations before we see godly leaders as outlined in scripture. In the long term, we will have better leaders, but the reality is we will still have bad and toxic leaders, despite our best efforts to circumvent this tendency. Lastly, the idea of having Nathans or Jonathans come alongside the leaders to give counsel and rebuke when necessary was raised. In response, it was stated that the Iranian churches may not be ready for this type of mentoring, which includes corrective criticism. In fact, within this culture, it is not permissible to criticise someone. The Iranian and Middle Eastern leadership model of authoritarianism is dominant. The problems have been recognized; now we must work toward solutions in order to see the development of mature, godly leaders.

6. Mediating Conflict Resolution: Can We All Just Get Along?

The goal of addressing conflict is to resolve the conflict and restore the relationship of the offended parties. Every culture has ways of dealing with conflict. One culture might use open confrontation, which is acceptable and culturally appropriate. In other cultures, open confrontation is viewed as dishonouring and aggressive. Both approaches can cause conflict. Therefore, mediation is necessary for dealing with conflict. However, the form mediation takes needs to reflect the cultural context.

There are two key ingredients in mediation: the mediator and the parties in conflict. In some cultures, the role of the mediator is focused on determining the guilty party without considering the impact that has on the people involved in the dispute. In other cultures, the mediator is to preserve the honour of both parties, while at the same time bringing the parties to a point of an acceptable resolution.

However, the offended parties also have a role to play, and the mediator may have little control over this aspect of mediation. The emotional maturity of the people in the dispute will determine the outcome of mediation. We will know if the mediation works if the offended parties stop the hostility or if those who have run away have returned. But we must go a step further. The goal of conflict resolution is to restore a relationship between the participants.

The cultural tendencies mentioned in the preceding chapters must also be taken into consideration. Drawing upon the insights of Geert Hofstede noted in Chapter 1, the combination of high-power distance, combined with high uncertainty avoidance (maintaining rigid codes of conduct), intolerance of unorthodox behaviours and ideas, and ranking as a restrained society, leads to a cultural pull to accept strong authoritarian leaders, who in turn control their members. All these cultural tendencies will shape the approach and possible outcomes of mediation.

All the previous topics on conflict, communication patterns, shame and chronic shame, and toxic and abusive leaders will shape the direction and outcome of mediation. Communication patterns complicate mediation. As noted in Chapter 2, there is direct and indirect communication. Indirect means the topic is circumvented until the mediator understands the root cause of the conflict. Communication patterns tend to use exaggeration to emphasise a point or to get attention. This can take hours before the topic is identified.

As we discussed in Chapter 2, shame is a dimension that needs to be taken into consideration. For instance, shame cultures must avoid shame at all costs. Shame must be hidden, so conflict can be left unnoticed for a long time. If shame is exposed, it must be avenged or denied. At all costs, honour must be restored. Therefore, keeping one's honour can hinder progress in mediation. People who have experienced chronic shame have an all-or-nothing approach to threats and hypersensitivity over perceived offenses, all of which complicate the task of the mediator.

But if the offended parties refuse to ever talk again or even be in the same space, there is something deeper that needs to be identified and resolved. If the offended parties are highly sensitive rather than secure in who they are, mediation will reflect parenting adult children. How do we overcome the problems of mediating conflicts in a culturally appropriate way that takes into consideration the complex cultural and individualistic response to conflict and conflict resolution? How can we reverse the trend of fellowships splitting or dissolving? How can we stabilise biblical unity through mediation in the cultural context so the church can bear much fruit?

Another dimension that complicates mediation is the strength and unity of the "ummah", the worldwide Muslim community, and how it plays an essential role in the individual identity of believers from a Muslim background. Belonging to *ummah* is where the BMBs feel security, acceptance, protection, and identity; so replacing that safe zone with another community brings assumptions. One assumption is that the experience in the new Christian community is what true ummah should look like. Mediation existed in the Middle East hundreds of years ago. In fact, the notion of deferring to a neutral and objective third party for a decision towards the resolution of a dispute is well-steeped in Arabic Islamic traditions. One story is about how Prophet Muhammad was chosen by feuding tribes to resolve a dispute around the reconstruction of the Ka'ba. He bridged the gap between the quarrelling parties and he himself suggested a solution that he saw as beneficial for all parties. Accordingly, Islamic Law (*Shari'a*) encourages this concept of an independent mediator through the practice of mediation (*Al Wasata*). *Al Wasata* is the practice of one or more persons intervening in a dispute, either at the request of one or both parties, or on their own initiative. The independent mediator attempts to resolve the dispute by proposing solutions to the parties, who are then free to determine if they want to accept the proposed solutions or not. That understanding defines the importance of mediation as an essential part of addressing conflict and how mediation is a cultural responsibility.

Another assumption is the role of the mediator. The status and reputation of the mediator are crucial in the Arab Islamic approach to mediation. The parties' respect for the mediator is very important for reaching applicable settlements. The mediator is perceived as someone who has all the answers and solutions. Consequently, the mediator plays an active role and takes an evaluative stance as opposed to the Western mediator who remains neutral and plays a facilitating role by allowing the disputants to reach a resolution by themselves.

While the Western mediator is more concerned with having knowledge about the legal procedures and structures, the mediator in the Middle East is required to know more about the history and facts of the conflict. Apart from the role and approach of the mediator, the goal is also different in the two contexts. In the

Middle East, it is important to continue the relationship between the parties and preserve social harmony in the group. In contrast, the Western mediator is focused on the maximisation of personal and group interests. The goal of the Middle Eastern mediator is to restore the broken relationship between the parties and within the community. The Western mediator views mediation as having a win/lose or win/win outcome, while the Middle Eastern mediator recognises the preservation of social harmony as a superordinate goal.

Middle Eastern mediation often takes place alongside a related formal legal proceeding while Western mediation takes place instead of formal legal proceedings. Although both approaches consider discretion essential to mediation, in the Middle East mediators may be summoned to a formal state court to testify about an agreement they have obtained.

Despite the positive historical and cultural background, the Middle East has not experienced a surge in the use of mediation institutions and processes. This is most likely because there are very few active and trained mediators in the region.

The first two presenters, an expatriate from the Iranian context followed by an expatriate from the Middle Eastern context, were asked to make a recorded 20-minute presentation on the topic of mediation to introduce the subject. What follows afterwards is the discussion that ensued from these first foundational presentations.

The Ministry of a Mediator – Expatriate in the Iranian Context

I have been a missionary at large to Farsi speaking people from 1994 to 2013. I am a pastor to the Iranian community and the Iranian Christian church of Colorado. I am on faculty and the board of directors for PARS Theological Center. In addition, I serve the Farsi-speaking world as a ministry coach and personal counsellor. I am the founder and executive director of Talim Ministries which produces, develops and distributes Biblical resources for Farsi-speaking leaders worldwide.

I have the privilege and honour to contribute on what it means to be a biblical mediator in the context of Persian culture. In this contribution, I will discuss the characteristics of a biblical mediator, and then examine some specific situations.

I am familiar with the Iranian church where a mediator was crucial in resolving the conflict. Our purpose is to understand mediation in the context of the Persian church.

The root meaning of the word mediator is "standing between" or "to be a person in between." My wife has some understanding of how the Cherokee Indians handle conflict. They take the two young people who are fighting and tie them to a tree. They leave them there until they are willing to make up. We do not tie people to trees today but, in a similar way, as Christians, we bring conflicting parties to the tree at Calvary, where Jesus brought reconciliation between God and man through his death and resurrection. This is the basis of our understanding of how meditation and reconciliation work. We want to take two people and bring them to the cross of Christ to experience His love and mercy.

We want them to understand that, as we have been greatly forgiven through Christ, so we are to forgive others (Eph. 4:32; Col. 3:13).

Peace-making or reconciliation is a commandment found in II Corinthians 5:18, stating that we all have been given the ministry of reconciliation. Whether you are a pastor or a layperson, as Christians we are called to mediate through prayer and encourage people who are in conflict to come together. We also know that we have Christ who is our perfect mediator, for scripture informs us that there is one mediator between God and man, and that is Jesus (I Tim. 2:5).

Jesus even used mediation before the cross. Let us consider Jesus' baptism. Jesus fully identified with our sins for he who knew no sin came forward to be baptised. This is a foretaste of Jesus completely identifying with us by becoming a mediator for us with God. The Bible is clear in John 14:6 that no one can come to the Father except through Christ. The DNA of Christian life is mediation. We are to be a holy nation that seeks to be peacemakers by bringing people together through our ministry of reconciliation. We are to be mediators.

Characteristics of a Mediator

The first characteristic we should look for in a mediator is a mature believer. Although maturity is important, in the Iranian context, the mature believer needs to have stature in the Iranian church community. This is someone with experience who is known as a person of integrity and really walks with the Lord. Iranians, especially older ones, say that they cannot accept the advice and wisdom of someone younger. This trait should not be that important in the church, but it is often the case in the culture. In seeking a mediator in our cultural context, we seek out a person of stature, someone who has proven to be a faithful Christian who loves Christ and the church. Another ingredient for the mature mediator is to be impartial in every way. In other words, they are not to have any say or profit in the outcome of the mediation. If they do have a conflict of interest, they need to make that clear from the very beginning. There should be a sense that the mediator loves and respects each party, whether two individuals or two groups in a church. The reputation of the mediator must be a person of absolute impartiality. I cannot underestimate the importance of this point.

The second characteristic of the mediator is to have the ability to understand the perspective of different people on an issue. This means that the mediator cannot be a black-and-white thinker. He/she/they must have the maturity and wisdom to know that two very committed Christians can have two very different opinions about the Bible, life, or a situation. To maintain an absolute neutral perspective, the mediator cannot put himself in the shoes of the other party. However, understanding the perspective of the other person is an important part of what the mediator does. Another quality of understanding differing perspectives requires the mediator to be a very good listener. This means not prejudging someone but truly giving each person the opportunity to fully explain their perspective. My practice is to give undivided time to each party to make their case. The first person is to share their perspective without any verbal reaction from the other person, contradicting statements, or emotional outbursts.

The moderator is to help the two parties to really listen to each other, both are given the opportunity to speak and be heard. An important aspect of mediation is to show empathy, emotional concern, and interest in what is going on in their lives. To do this adequately, the moderator should be grounded in grace because this is a situation in which grace is so needed. Grace is needed for the mediator since they may well experience tension, anger, rejection, or accusations as they try to mediate between the parties.

So, as a mediator, you need to be a person grounded in grace, under the control of the Holy Spirit, able to speak calmly and softly to angry people, and help them settle down. You will also need to introduce grace to them. We will cover that later. Mediation is going through the process with the eye on grace, that you both are sinners, needing forgiveness. Both have at least offended the other in some way and it is not all the other person's fault.

The third characteristic of a mediator is to be a wise person, having biblical wisdom and knowledge of God's word and how to apply it. The mediator should have a reservoir of biblical examples in their heart and mind of how to illustrate reconciliation and forgiveness. Wisdom begins with the fear of God and grows as the Christian truly learns to walk with God to apply the scriptures, and to have life experiences to draw upon. People want a mediator who has been down this road before and knows what they are doing.

The final characteristic of a mediator is to be trusted by both sides. I want to know that they will trust my opinion and perspective, and take serious consideration to act upon it. There is no point in going through all the effort of mediation just for the sake of saying that they went through this mediation, but nothing has changed in their relationship. I ask for a serious commitment, and I want them to trust me and trust God. I want them to know that I am going to do the very best I can to make this work. None of us are perfect mediators, but an important component is the heart of the mediator.

Being a mediator is a very big responsibility. We do it on our knees in prayer, carefully and thoughtfully. We accept this role even though sometimes it is a very difficult responsibility.

Mediation in the Persian Context

In a shame/honour culture, there are many different things that can upset people, such as insults, lack of respect, and shaming. Conflicts can flare up very quickly in the Iranian church. The root of much of it is pride. Conflicts lead to people avoiding each other, which is the first stage. They often refuse to speak to each other. For example, one Iranian brother told me that the person who hurt him was dead to him and didn't exist to him anymore. Another reaction is rebuke. Iranians can be very outspoken in their criticism. I have had Iranians come to church and rebuke me in front of everybody with the purpose to shame me, but they ended up shaming themselves. This can cause even more divisions. Revenge can happen, beginning with gossip, spreading a negative perspective of the opponent, and alienating others. It is not unusual to hear that an offended person asks their friends not to deal with the other person even if they are friends. This behaviour is on full display in the church, and it is very painful, causing division and splits in the church. It is a very serious issue that needs our attention.

From my experience, there are four models that show how mediation works:

1. The first model for the mediator is to initiate contact or dialogue between two people who are alienated. This has happened to me. One very kind Iranian brother called me saying, "You know so-and-so is very upset with you." I couldn't quite understand why. After the reasons were given, I realised that I had come to his town and did not have time to speak with him. He was upset that I had not reached out to him, so he was hurt. This mediator prompted me to call that brother and to apologise for my neglect that this had happened. I called him and told him that I hoped that the next time I came to town, I would see him. This phone call healed our relationship. The work of the mediator, in this case, was to bring two people together and encourage an apology, even though one of them didn't even know that he had offended the other person. Sometimes, the mediator must take a proactive role and initiate the dialogue.
2. The second model of mediation is when two individuals are in conflict. I had two elders in the church who were against each other, who criticised each other, and were unable to cope with each other. I called them both into my office. They did not ask for mediation. I sat them down, locked the door to my office, and said, "We are not going anywhere until we resolve this problem." I read scripture to them for a while and then I prayed. Then I said, "I want you to begin to tell me how you have sinned in this relationship. I don't want you to talk about the other person at all. I will ask the Holy Spirit to show you where you were wrong, not the other brother." We prayed and it was quite a little while, then one of the brothers said that he knew that he had been a very proud person and he had not allowed his brother to express himself without criticising him. Then, the other brother began to talk about his part in the conflict. The result was that they asked each other for forgiveness. It was a powerful experience. From that point, they were good friends again. They couldn't work it out themselves; instead, they needed a mediator. The Iranian pride culture and their own personal pride didn't allow them to address the conflict on their own. When individuals in the church experience conflict, the leaders of the church will have to intervene between the warring parties to move toward forgiveness and reconciliation.
3. The third model of mediation is when two Iranian brothers are in business together. Unfortunately, Iranians typically go into business together without signing any contract with the details of their arrangement. With the passing of time, the relationship deteriorates. In this particular case, the relationship had deteriorated to the point where large sums of money were owed and one partner was suffering financially. I called them into my office and closed the door and we sat at a table. I asked each person to share his perspective of what had happened, what had gone wrong, and anything they felt they did wrong in the business. They were not too eager to share

what they did wrong, but they did share about their business and all the problems that they were experiencing. I was taking notes and, just like in a court hearing, we went back and forth until I was able to come up with a suggestion based on the facts. There was forgiveness and apologies were extended; they were able to walk out of the room as reconciled brothers. After we have intervened through mediation in a conflict, we may never really know if there is true forgiveness when the parties walk out of that room. We trust they left without anger or a feeling that they were abused in the process or that justice wasn't done. That is the hard part. We did our best and I felt that we came to some kind of resolution. This relationship was tearing the church apart. That is why I discourage brothers and sisters in the church from going into business together because, so often, it leads to problems. A mediator was necessary. By stepping in, we were able to ward off a bigger problem that would have affected the whole church.

4. The fourth model of mediation is when there is a serious church split. This is much harder to deal with and restore. Several years ago, I was called to a congregation that was split – 2/3 versus 1/3. I quickly discerned the reason was over very distinct theological differences that could not be resolved. It is difficult when an Iranian church comes together, not because they are all Iranians, but because they come from multiple theological backgrounds. Because they do not have a common theological foundation, splits and divisions are bound to occur. In addition to different theological differences, there are different leadership styles. One style of leadership is the more democratic church polity built upon an egalitarian worldview, often found in charismatic churches. The other popular church polity is the traditional authoritative leader built upon the hierarchical worldview. In the Iranian church in the West, there is the merging of the two cultures, with old-time leaders and new-time leaders who naturally will have conflicts. There is a lot of spiritual pride in these situations. I quickly noticed that each had built up their own cheerleading gallery that supported their preferred style of leadership. It became obvious that this church was going to split. There wasn't much that I could do. I tried to bring some peace by meeting with the different groups, entreating them about preserving the glory of God and the church. Unfortunately, this church did split and each group suffered the consequences.

It is important to understand that, for Persian culture, mediation is a critical ingredient and ministry in many cases because of the nature of the culture. It could be between two people in the church who have a conflict and mediation is the only way to save face. Marriage is another area that greatly needs help. I have stepped in and tried to mediate between many marriages. It makes sense for us to spend the energy and time to train young pastors in the art of mediation using biblical patterns. We cannot stop the interpersonal conflicts, the theological conflicts, or the ministry conflicts, but we can be prepared to help those facing these conflicts so that their church will be empowered to stand in the gap through mediation.

Reconciliation and Mediation –
Expatriate in the Middle East & North Africa

I am the director for International Theological Education Network. I have lived twenty-eight years in four different countries around the Mediterranean: France, Morocco, Egypt, and Lebanon. My focus has been on discipleship and leadership development in the Muslim context. My contribution will focus on two areas: 1) prerequisites for reconciliation and mediation, and 2) the qualities of a mediator.

Prerequisites for Reconciliation and Mediation

There are four prerequisites which we need to consider when working toward reconciliation through mediation.

First, acknowledge that there is a conflict. This may seem obvious but think about it with me for a moment. Saying that "I am hurt" is difficult. You expose yourself and you feel vulnerable. When I say, "I am hurt", it makes me look weak. What if the other person says that I'm only imagining it? What if they don't validate my pain? Then you feel isolated. We live in cultures that operate on a basis of shame and honour. Admitting our pain is difficult because it makes us feel ashamed.

But there can never be any progress if we can't acknowledge that we're hurt. In the Middle East, we would say "*ma'alesh*" (no problem). It's a way of brushing aside what happened as though it doesn't matter. Notice the difference when I say "*ana hasis bi-alam*" (I feel pain), or "*ana majruh*" (I am wounded). The first, "*ma'alesh*", is a way of brushing aside hurt and bitterness. Of course, those wounds don't just go away! The second, "*ana hasis bi-alam*" is an acknowledgement, a plea for help. It owns the pain and expresses a need. I need help to get better. To say that you must feel secure in your relationship with the person who hurt you. There must be a baseline of trust between you and that person. That's not easy when there has been a history of conflict. Trust must be restored, which may mean seeking help from a mediator – a third party who helps in the process of communication.

Second, we must own the hurt that we've inflicted. How do you respond when someone says to you, "You hurt me?" "I didn't mean to!" But that sidesteps the issue and fails to own it and accept responsibility for your part in it. In effect, it's saying, "It's your fault because you misunderstood." When we care for the other person, we have to set aside our desire to justify ourselves and to defend what we've done. The issue is not what you intended. The issue is how it was received. What did the person feel? If we know ourselves well and think about ourselves as the Bible defines us, we can understand that we may say or do things which hurt others. We shouldn't be too surprised when that happens; we should be willing to listen carefully and quietly when someone tells us that something we have done has hurt them.

Third, keep confidentialities. We must stop talking to other parties about the hurt between us. Proverbs says that "in a multitude of words, sin thrives" (Prov. 10:19). The more we talk to others about the conflict, the more words grow and the deeper the wounds become. Stop talking! Mediators who do their work well give us a place to express our hurt and frustration. They, as well, need to commit to confidentiality – keeping the offense private.

I've lived in the Middle East and North Africa for a long time, and I know that this is not the way our culture works. When we are hurt, it's very hard not to share that with the people around us. It is essential to love our brothers and sisters in Christ. Even though we are hurt, we must believe in the best of our brothers and sisters. We must keep the hurt between us, refusing to release the poison of gossip into our fellowships and churches. That commitment will greatly increase the likelihood of mediation and reconciliation.

Fourth, we must have empathy. If conflicts are going to be resolved, we must be willing to put ourselves in the skin of the other person. We must make every effort to see things as they see them. This is incredibly hard on our old selfish ego. But it is exactly what Jesus did for us. He took on human skin, a human body, to effect reconciliation for us. If we love our brothers and sisters, we have to learn to see things through their eyes, to feel things with their emotions.

Mediation and the Qualities of a Mediator

Interpersonal conflicts are difficult. We often need a third party, a mediator, to help us work through them. This is the point of Matthew 18. Jesus says that if someone has sinned against us, we are to go to them in private and tell them what has happened. If they listen and reconciliation takes place, well and good. But if they don't listen, Jesus says to take one or two others with you. Jesus instructs us to bring in a third party in difficult situations.

People who can mediate conflict are a gift to Christ's body. Perhaps you could become peacemakers in Christ's body in the Muslim world. We need that desperately. These are some qualifications for a mediator:

1. A mediator should be acceptable to both sides of a conflict. Mediators are trusted people. In other words, this person is not partisan. They are not inherently biased toward one person or the other. This means the mediator is able to separate themself from the conflict to look at it objectively. They are not seeking approval from the two parties in the conflict. They are secure in themselves, so they don't depend on others' approval for their sense of worth. They know themselves to be a child of God, dearly loved. Although such people often have a status in the church, their value is not derived from their status in the community, but from being a child of God. As such, they are trustworthy.

2. A mediator should be a person of wisdom. Finding a person of wisdom is rare and valuable. They should have theological wisdom. They know that sin is bound deeply in the heart and that getting it out and dealing with it can be very challenging. It means they are not "shocked" by a deep conflict. They know human nature and expect conflict. They also have interpersonal wisdom. They know how to listen empathetically, and they also can help the two offended parties listen to each other. Often, good mediators are people who have passed through suffering themselves, so they know how to feel

the pain of others, but not lose their own sense of personhood. They don't become so enmeshed in the pain of another that they lose their objectivity.
3. The mediator has the skills of mediation. There are certain steps and skills in mediation that are recognised:
   a. Defining the source of the conflict. This requires careful listening and leading the two parties to agree on precisely when the conflict began and what circumstances have added stress to the relationship. Often, a conflict began weeks or months before the breakage happened in the relationship through a thoughtless word that has now grown to become a mountain of conflict. There are often deep roots to interpersonal conflict.
   b. Eliciting a strategy for resolution: the mediator needs to lead the two parties in suggesting words and actions which will heal the broken relationship. Are there apologies that need to be offered? Do behaviours need to change? Does material or financial reparation need to be made? If one person has been harmed emotionally, physically, or materially, how does the other person make a genuine reparation for that harm? The mediator has the skills to lead both parties to an agreement on how the harm can be repaired and hopefully healed.
   c. Suggesting new ways of engaging interpersonally: the mediator helps the two conflicted parties take steps toward each other so that the relationship can be healed and trust restored. This may take time and require small steps over long periods of time. Trust needs to be rebuilt, which is not easy, but the objective is that the relationship is restored with the two parties agreeing to become friends, love each other, and remain in communication. In so many conflicts I've seen, the two parties never speak to each other. If one is in a meeting, the other won't attend. That's not reconciliation, that's perpetuating a conflict. Even if the steps are small, we need to move toward reconciliation.
   d. Keeping confidentialities: the parties must be confident that once a resolution is agreed upon, the mediator does not talk about what happened. The agreement is confidential. Not causing shame is important. If the conflict is talked about or brought up in a sermon or used as an example, it can bring a lot of shame to the parties in conflict. Sometimes, a conflict is big enough that a whole church is impacted. In that case, it may be important that the reconciliation is communicated publicly.

The mediator is not responsible for ending the conflict. That responsibility is on the conflicted parties. They are the ones who must change words and actions and begin to live with trust toward one another.

Application

Our reflexes are almost always wrong in regard to conflict. The usual ways in which we react to conflict are fight or flight (running away).

The Apostle Paul had conflict with the Apostle Peter, described in Galatians 2:11-21. Paul confronted Peter for withdrawing from table fellowship with the Gentiles because some Jews had come from Jerusalem. It must have been serious because Paul said that Peter, the rock upon whom Jesus would build the church, was not acting in accordance with the gospel. This is almost unimaginable that the Rock of the church, Peter, betrayed the gospel.

But I believe Peter must have accepted that confrontation because 1) the church of Antioch didn't split into a Peter Church and a Paul Church, and 2) because when Peter wrote his final epistle, he spoke about Paul's letters as "scripture" or the word of God (2 Pet. 3:14-18). Since Peter had this conflict and was able to accept correction and guard the unity of the body of Christ, we should be like him and preserve the unity of Christ's body even through conflict.

Synopsis of Discussions

The following summarises the panel discussion and the eight breakout room conversations on this topic, dealing with mediation in the Middle Eastern context. We begin with the Arab context and later will listen to the insights of Iranians.

I like what the second presenter had to say about the mentor, but practically speaking, is it possible to have someone impartial to both sides? It is typical for someone to wonder if the mediator is truly impartial.

That is a good point. A lot of my friends will project their presupposition onto the other person, even if the mediator is neutral. The offended parties are projecting questions like, "What will the mediator gain? Who are they? Why should they be able to mediate in this dispute?" Another difficulty could be if you are the one bringing this person to mediate, will they side with you? It could be difficult even to agree on who should mediate. But within a church, it may be different, like in the first presenter's scenario in which it was the pastor and two people in the church having a disagreement. So, it is important for the pastor to foster trust through the relationships he/she develops within the church.

Mediation is Complicated: I like the different examples the first speaker presented to us. For instance, in one situation, the offended parties act proactively to seek the help of a mediator. Rarely is mediation simply to determine who has been wronged and a solution found to restore the relationship. I see mediation as being very complicated. It is more than just bringing people together since conflict needs extraordinary wisdom to unravel the subtle root causes of any conflict. For example, the situation could be that both parties are at fault, for they have made the conflict worse. Mediation in this case is a very painful job. The mediator must rebuke both parties to help them see how badly they have behaved since both parties are wrong. Great wisdom and courage are needed to bring the parties to the point of recognising their deep sin. It's not an easy job. Another scenario is when both parties are partially right and telling the truth. The mediator must help the offended parties to see that they partly understand the truth, but the whole truth needs a wider perspective

Mediation becomes even more difficult when the mediator is dealing with the same issues they are asked to address. The reconciler first needs to ask for forgiveness of their sin before asking the conflicting parties to seek forgiveness. The hardest situation is when it is impossible to recognise the main issue causing the conflict. People can be so deceptive. For example, in one case, I heard the grievances and rendered my judgement in favour of one person. Then, the other person got offended. Later, details came out that were omitted when they told their stories. In the end, it was impossible to be certain of the facts. We as mediators and counsellors can be so easily deceived.

We have talked about three areas. First, communication styles. Instead of direct communication, indirect communication is used. With indirect communication, there are nuances that are hard to pick up, so we don't know exactly what is being communicated. Second, how do we mediate when addressing an issue that will cause shame? For instance, if the person is suffering from chronic shame and is deeply hurt, it doesn't matter what the offense is, they will experience shame. Third, if there is any toxicity in the relationship, it adds another layer of complexity when seeking reconciliation.

We need Stories and Examples: First, I feel that both presenters were phenomenal, giving beautiful details and highlighting the various dynamics of reconciliation. But I think examples and stories were lacking. In our group in the last session, we were very candid and honest that we did not have successful Nathan stories [the prophet and counsellor of King David] in our lives and ministries. I would love to hear stories of reconciliation. I think we need more of that. I'm not talking about husband/wife reconciliation, but about church conflict and leader conflict. Do we have successful stories? We can have beautiful theories, principles, psychological insights, and biblical passages, but we need actual stories of how reconciliation has worked out.

Having examples and resources will be very important. Francis Schaeffer's little book, *The Mark of a Christian*, talks about the sense of unity and love among Christians based upon what Jesus says in John 13:35 and 17:23, "By this everyone will know that you are my disciples if you love one another." "I in them and you in me – so that they are brought to complete unity. Then the world will know that you sent me and have loved them even as you have loved me." That little book gives two examples of love and unity. One is about a church in Germany. Half of the congregation compromised with Hitler and were not persecuted. The other half went underground and some were martyred. Then after WWII, they met and prayed together, repented, and became one.

The other example on the surface didn't seem very successful. A traditional congregation had a young hippy generation coming into it; each group didn't get along very well, so they decided to split with the support and blessing of each other. These are concrete examples of one that was a success story and another of how things didn't work out the way they wanted. But they can still love and support each other while parting and blessing each other. I would like to suggest that, for future endeavours, we have more role models and case studies of reconciliation.

Mediation and Forgiveness: I have some questions about reconciliation. Is mediation connecting two leaders to stay and work with each other, or should they even be brought back together? Should the leaders just forgive each other and not have any hatred or anger in their hearts towards each other? Or should we force them to reconnect in their work and ministries? Does mediation mean reconnecting and serving with each other, or does it mean forgiving each other and protecting their hearts from bitterness? They may forgive each other, but they might not continue to work together.

We have talked a lot about mediation and reconciliation. In my experience, the issue is more about forgiveness. The weaker person in the church is the one who leaves, and the other one stays. I've been trying to think about success stories, but generally, the people go their separate ways. Going two different ways is fine, but forgiveness is important. Let's make sure that forgiveness happens. In the Arab context, this is more difficult than anything I've faced before. Forgiveness is a big issue.

Do we have good examples of church leaders or issues that you felt were truly reconciled where those in conflict resolved their issues and continued to walk together on the same path? I have more examples of forgiveness, but going separate ways. They come to the point where they choose by God's grace to forgive their hurt and let go of it. On a local church level, I have seen people continue to work together. But when you have inter-church situations, that is much more difficult. What is needed is being a part of a structure like a Presbytery or a church structure which calls them to continue to be in a working relationship. I agree that the first goal should be to forgive, release, and be able to accept the brother. But sometimes you cannot work with people because of theological differences or style differences. That's okay. It is crucial to work toward forgiveness. I do a lot of teaching on forgiveness because this is such a misunderstood topic. Forgiveness is different than reconciliation. Reconciliation is when two people can become good friends, but that doesn't always work out. I do have examples of heroic stories of mediation working through my own ministry.

Iranian Experience with Mediation: I would like to share something about Iranian culture and context. People will ask you to help them with reconciliation and, because of our culture, they will look to the leader as a fatherly figure who typically supports them. During the conflict, both parties want the mediator to side with them. When you take a neutral position of truth and justice, and you confront someone, saying they must ask for forgiveness from the other party, the other party will be offended. From a cultural perspective of looking for a fatherly figure to intervene, the expectations Iranians have for the leader are not realistic. They don't expect the arbitrator to be objective when taking the case. Both parties expect that the mediator will support their perspective. These expectations place the arbitrator into a difficult no-win situation.

For example, I was friends with both parties when they asked me to mediate between them. After making my recommendation, they both said they didn't expect that kind of rendering from me. The cultural expectation is to find someone who will support their position. This is the pressure we Iranian pastors are put into. The pastor is pressured so that he is unable to judge between people logically or impartially. As a friend, you can't go against the friendship with a just ruling.

In one case, a group suffered at the hand of abusive leaders. It was impossible to talk to them about the abuse because they were so traumatised. Since we couldn't talk to them about the trauma, we suggested that they think about forgiveness. Finally, this group forgave their leaders. When there is trauma, you can't expect people to come to the point of reconciliation. The best-case scenario is to achieve forgiveness.

The Need for Resources on Mediation: I'm familiar with two resources; Ken Sande wrote *The Peace Maker: A Biblical Guide to Resolving Personal Conflict* and I recently taught Charles Stanley's *The Gift of Forgiveness* on satellite TV. But, in terms of the real dynamics of mediation and reconciliation, we don't have a lot of resources that address the cultural sensitivity that our first contributor was talking about, or the complexities raised in this chapter.

Culturally, if you are a friend, you need to take sides, you can't be a neutral mediator. That is not acceptable in our culture. In arbitrating a conflict, some of our fatherly, loving, gracious church leaders passed down harsh verdicts. The psychological sensitivity and empathy for both sides are not there. The result is that people are really hurt, and people leave the church. We need really good resources. This may be a topic on which some of our Western leaders might not be as helpful as some of our own more culturally sensitive Christian workers.

Several years ago, I read a book on the Armenian genocide. The setting was a delegation of Armenians who went to Turkey in an effort to bring reconciliation between Armenians and Turks, which is inconceivable in our Armenian culture. Any Armenian who would venture to do this would be labelled a betrayer of the nation and would face all-out rejection. Armenians believe that Turks committed what could be called "crimes against humanity" to our nation. Rafi Shahverdyan wrote the book *Armenian Wine, Turkish Bread: A Real-Life Journey of Reconciliation*. It is about the journey that these brave Armenians took to Turkey to start a conversation with evangelical church pastors there. The Armenian delegation asked for forgiveness because they were full of hatred against the Turks. In response, the Turkish pastors asked for forgiveness from the Armenians because their forefathers massacred their people. In that exchange between two groups of Christians, something special happened. Reconciliation was achieved through the courage the Armenians took to initiate this risky venture. Brother Rafi was criticised by some Armenian pastors for what he participated in. He was accused of going to a foreign country where the killers of their forefathers were. These Armenian pastors were under a lot of pressure, not from the Turkish Christians, but from the Turkish nationalists. One person in the Armenian delegation was taken by the Turkish nationalists to be killed. This is an example of entering into what was considered a cultural and national taboo.

For an Armenian, it can be unimaginable to connect with a Turk. Many years ago, I met with a Turkish brother who has a Ph.D. from Cambridge. His dissertation was on the Armenian genocide. He is an evangelical brother who was a Turkish Christian activist tackling the Armenian genocide. There must have been a tremendous amount of pressure against him from his fellow Turks since he was trying to defend the Armenians. The aim of his academic work was to bring reconciliation between the two nations. In his dissertation, he called the genocide a crime against the Armenians. Sometimes, the issues are so very sensitive that it is nearly impossible to approach the subject. There is a lot of emotional trauma associated with the event of the Armenian genocide. In mediation, there is personal trauma and sometimes national trauma, as in this case.

Some of the books on shame culture address the topic of mediation. A couple years ago, I was asked to do a seminar for TCI (a Christian television broadcaster in Italy) on reconciliation within a shame culture. I did an extensive study on the topic and found out that there are two issues. There are theological and biblical issues and issues of how to work that through the culture. I came to the realisation that the Bible is written in a shame culture. Many of the illustrations in the Old and New Testaments talk about how reconciliation can take place. For example, the way Jesus honoured Zacchaeus, who was a hated person, by sharing the gospel with him, which led to him becoming a believer. I didn't find a particular book on this topic, but when you get into some of the literature about shame/honour cultures, you find hidden segments and treasures about how to do reconciliation and mediation.

I keep coming back to the idea that we need stories. We need inspiration. This is a huge piece of the puzzle. I was one of the translators at Billy Graham's conference in Amsterdam in 2000. There were fifty people from Iran from various churches and different denominational spectrums. They were not on good speaking terms with each other. I was translating a session about the Jim Elliot missionary group who were martyred in Ecuador. The son of one of the missionaries was there with two or three Auca Indians who had killed the missionaries. One of them said, "This man baptised me; he is the pastor of the church and I'm an elder."

I was passionately translating this for the Iranians coming from different denominations who were not even talking to each other. I enthusiastically affirmed this story that if this man can have this kind of relationship with the people who murdered his father, we must do better as a Christian community. By the end of that conference, the relationship was much better among various Christian Iranian leaders, not just because of that testimony, but because of a whole host of things. We need heroic stories. Pope Francis washed the feet of some prisoners, who included some Muslims, in a pre-Easter service near Rome in April 2019. That was so inspiring that a prominent Iranian activist, a Shite Muslim in Iran, went to the home of a Baha'i family and washed the feet of Baha'i children whose parents had been imprisoned by the Islamic regime.

We need inspiration. We need models of how these principles are applied. One evening, I was doing a segment for TV on the topic of Malcolm Gladwell, one of the most prolific writers of our time; he had left his Christian faith, but had come back to it. While working on a book, he met a Christian family in Canada who had forgiven and loved the person who had raped and murdered their daughter. To see that this can happen in the life of human beings, this kind of love, forgiveness, and reconciliation greatly impacted him and brought him back to the Christian faith. The importance of models to encourage the Christian community is a huge need as people are thinking about producing resources.

Currently in the US, there is a big discussion about black/white reconciliation because of shootings, discrimination, and the legacy of slavery. Glen Kehrein and Raleigh Washington wrote *Breaking Down Walls: A Model for Reconciliation in an Age of Racial Strife,* which talks about reconciliation between the black and white communities. Would these stories, although they are not Middle Eastern in context, be the kind of books to translate into either Arabic or Farsi?

I would say yes. To my shame, I saw a documentary on PBS on the black church a few months ago, and I realised how much we need stories of the black church in Iran. Stories of their resilience and faithfulness amid oppression and injustice are something we need to hear. I feel like the persecuted church needs to know a lot more about the black church in America.

Yes, every story regarding forgiveness and reconciliation speaks to our hearts regardless of the cultural background. What the African Americans experienced is horrible and they give us many lessons we need to learn. We need stories that are real. For example, ten years ago, the wife of a Christian brother in Iran left him. She didn't even talk to him about leaving. She left this dear brother, taking their child with her, and married the man with whom she had an affair. This man shared with me that he had forgiven his wife for what she did. That was an unbelievable story of grace and forgiveness which impacted me. But the story doesn't end there. This second marriage seemed to go well, but after some years, her second husband divorced her. This Christian woman was left in a very difficult situation financially, with two children, one from the first marriage and one from the second marriage. Divorced women in Iran are left in a very precarious situation without the means to survive. In desperation, she reached out to her first husband for financial help. He didn't hesitate and took on monthly financial support so she could live. He didn't remarry her, but financially helped her. Jesus can really change people's hearts. This is a good example of Christian forgiveness and reconciliation.

One of the witnesses that impacted my friends in the Gulf region was the story of the 20 Egyptian Coptic Christian construction workers who were executed by beheading on 21st February 2015, on a beach in Libya near Sirte. The mothers, brothers, and sisters testified that they forgave the ISIS terrorists for this execution, recalling Jesus' words from the cross that they forgave the perpetrators because they didn't know what they were doing.

I will give you another example. I mentioned Raleigh Washington and the black-and-white racial situation. I was recently at a conference in which Raleigh Washington spoke about his story of reconciliation in the past. At the end of his message, he got down on his knees and asked for forgiveness from his white brothers, because his black brothers have painted all the whites as racist just because they are white. Dr Washington said, "On behalf of all the blacks, please forgive us." He said that the narrative has totally shifted, accusing all whites of being oppressors because of the colour of their skin. This was a turning point of the conference.

The Effect of Trauma on Mediation: When the trauma and hurt are so deep, it does not allow for forgiveness to take place. One of the things that we are involved in is how to minister to the Afghans who are coming to the US. The number one issue we must deal with is trauma counselling. Once we are able to address their trauma and bring them through the steps of trauma, that then releases them to begin to consider forgiveness and reconciliation. Going through the layers of the pain is like peeling an onion. Layers must come off before we can get to the point of forgiveness and reconciliation. In the context of trauma, are we saying that there are some things that we cannot address until we address trauma first, by going through trauma healing?

Exactly! Psychologically, it is impossible for someone to even talk or think about forgiveness and reconciliation. Their traumatic experience presses so much into their subconscious that the person can be so full of hatred. The place to begin is with deep trauma therapy, which takes time. You need to help the person process all those negative emotions by talking through and expressing them. Often the person needs more than just talking about the trauma, it also needs to be expressed. This can be done through art therapy or psychodrama and other therapies. After this long process of trauma healing, the person comes to the point where they can begin to think about what has happened to them. It is at this point that we can introduce forgiveness. Without this process, all our efforts are useless. It is only after walking a person through deep long-term trauma therapy that the traumatised person can determine if they want to forgive or not.

If trauma is one of the factors preventing forgiveness and reconciliation, how do we tackle this obstacle? Since so many Christians in this region of the world are traumatised by the Islamic authoritarian regime or the heavy hand of totalitarian leaders or failed states, does everyone need trauma counselling? Are we chasing conflict in this consultation without addressing the root cause?

I don't think that everyone needs trauma counselling. As a nation, Iranians are traumatised. But I read that statistically many people who confront tragic events are not personally affected and traumatised by them because of factors that make them resilient. Not everyone is traumatised in the psychological sense of the term. I do believe that trauma is a huge factor but, so far, we have not incorporated it into our discipleship. It needs to be addressed at the level of discipleship. Sometimes, trauma gets addressed when people talk about shame. But I feel that we have not been very perceptive about the role of trauma, and how it affects our discipleship, preaching, counselling, and leadership development. This is my new emerging conviction; I believe it is something we should consider.

I completely agree. In our discipleship, we need to consider dealing with trauma. One dimension is when church members suffer from trauma and how it impacts the relationships within the church. But a dimension we also need to address is when a leader has experienced deep trauma. How will this impact the future of the church? Unfortunately, I personally know leaders who suffer from trauma, and you can see the effects of that trauma in the way the leader interacts with the members. I know church members who have been deeply damaged because of the leader, and no one is listening to them. The reason for this silence is that the leader is a charismatic leader who preaches well. The traumatised leader can be a good teacher, have good intellectual abilities, and have a good grasp on philosophical issues, but in personal relationships, the leader wounds people. I see that the greater danger is when some people in leadership roles are suffering from trauma. Some people might object that a person in leadership can be struggling from a trauma. But it is possible. A quick survey of history will reveal that leaders of nations can also lead through their trauma. For example, Adolf Hitler and Joseph Stalin were traumatised when growing up, but because of their intellect and leadership abilities, they became powerful leaders of their countries. Predictably, they created disasters in the Second World War.

Screening for Toxic or Traumatised Leaders: Another aspect that is just as important is how to prevent people suffering from unresolved trauma from coming into leadership in the church. I would suggest that we need to come up with some preventive screening so that can identify potentially abusive leaders and block the pathway to leadership in the church for those who use their trauma to harm others. Sadly, the only criteria that we have for our leaders is their ability to be good preachers, teachers, and evangelists. An important dimension to also consider is relational, in how the leader interacts with others. I see within the Farsi-speaking churches that we have leaders suffering from trauma.

Money and Power in Mediation: There are a couple of things we need to pay attention to. In our previous session, there was a discussion about the role of money and power in creating issues of toxicity. We have been very silent about money. Money and power are two major topics, which in these two days, we have not yet talked about. When we are talking about the context of reconciliation, sometimes there is jealousy, rivalry, and tension because there is power and money in the middle. I am thinking about a church in Turkey where the leadership fell apart, in part because of jealousy and rivalry over the sources of money.

Recommendations for Future Consultations: First, the issues of power and money need to be addressed. Second, we need to address the issue of justice when we talk about conflict and reconciliation. The element of justice was missing in talking about the conflict between the two parties in these discussions.

This reminds me of a situation we had in a church where some Muslim-background Arabs were joking, and said to another Muslim-background Arab, "When we joined this church, they gave us this amount of money, so why didn't they give it to you?" They were joking, for they hadn't received any money. That little joke led to a big headache of conflict and a split in the church. Money and power, even if it is a joke, can cause a lot of issues.

Resource: Richard Foster's book, *Money, Sex and Power: The Challenge of the Disciplined Life*, should be translated into Farsi if it hasn't been already.

> Switching from Arab to Iranian voices as we continue exploring mediation in the Middle Eastern context.

A Way Forward: No matter to what extent a mediator is an expert in his work and has unique experience, and no matter how much both parties want to make peace, sometimes the root of the dispute is so deep that we cannot agree on things. It is rooted in our worldview and life experiences. So, I think the problem existing in the churches is that we don't have a clear strategy to deal with things that could not be agreed upon and say, "What is the next step?"

Mary Dinsmore Ainsworth was an American-Canadian developmental psychologist known for her work in the development of attachment theory. In her book *Strange Situation*, she identifies three interesting conditions in people's personalities:

1. People are secure in their personalities
2. They are worried/anxious
3. They are either preventative or avoidant

In her guidebook, she shows how these personality types forgive, how they look at issues, how they make peace, and how they look at God. That is, the way we forgive, make peace, and understand God is different. For example, people who have avoidant characteristics (#3), no matter what you do, they often don't forgive or it is very hard for them to forgive. People with a secure personality (#1) easily hear, think, and accept the opposite opinion.

I think that what is very important is that we, as mediators, should pay attention to the personality of the parties in the conflict, and consider the way that they deal with and react in crises, the opposition and tension they show, and the appropriate response to it.

My personal observation is that we Iranians who have experienced war have avoidant characteristics. That is why we find it hard to forgive. There are other people who experienced serious crises, such as war and famine, and they, like us, go into prevention and avoidance mode to save their lives. We have experienced this in Iran for eight years.

Maybe this is one of the reasons that we Middle Easterners are hard to forgive because we have faced hard crises in our lifetime. I believe that we still need healing so we can experience conflict resolution. After we have been healed, we can deal with people better.

What Types of People Are Worried or Anxious? People who are always worried or anxious see the crisis as much worse than it really is. Their assessment of the situation is exaggerated, and they overreact to the situation. The response is not suitable for that situation. For example, someone asked someone else to get up from a chair and sit on another chair. The person being asked to move calls this disrespectful and says that the other meant to disrespect him. It was a simple request, but the person's reaction was inappropriate in that case.

Anxious people can make a Bible study tense. The Bible study leader tells the group to open the word of God together. But the anxious person comes with a lens which tells them that God is not a safe place for them, and they see God as a danger. Therefore, the minute we want to read the word with them, we must take into consideration how they view God and respond to it appropriately.

Show Transparency: The role of the mediator is to observe a certain amount of transparency. When and if they see progress in resolving the dispute, then they can share their own testimony of dealing with identical issues or problems in their life. By expressing such issues, they can help speed up the healing process.

I will give you an example. There was a father in the church who had a problem with his son for 20 years and did not talk to him. He suffered a lot and said that he couldn't forgive his son because he had destroyed all his property. I talked to him about my personal experience in a similar case of how I forgave the person and healing came into my life.

When I told him this, his heart softened a bit and we prayed together, and he entered the healing process. This took time and his life changed. There was a lot of pain endured by this father during those years that he could not communicate with his own son.

The problems in the church are not usually related to member-to-member; rather, they may have problems with their families. There was a case where a person had a problem with his brother. In another case, a dear woman hated her mother and could not forgive her. We share our personal experiences with them so that they know that we sympathise with them and understand that we don't just want to give them a prescription. This way can help them enter into the process of healing or forgiveness to solve those problems more easily.

Experience Forgiveness before Mediating: Sometimes, people want to make fun of us pastors who have not forgiven other people for years, and this creates other problems. There is a proverb that says: "If you were a doctor, you would treat yourself." How is it that a person cannot forgive others and at the same time wants to become a mediator to reconcile two other people?

We have a lot of rooted issues in our upper-class leadership groups who have carried such burdens for years. When they talk about their wounds, one can see the anger in them. Such people cannot be successful people in the church. It is very good for us to first experience forgiveness and then become a mediator to teach others the act of forgiveness.

Healing Is Needed: I agree that all the leaders and members of the church should be in the process of healing because everyone has problems. I don't think that there is a leader or member who does not have these problems or issues related to a lack of forgiveness. We must constantly evaluate and test ourselves.

Need to Learn Conflict Resolution: From all these presentations, we realise how necessary it is for us to learn and teach the principles and techniques of mediation. There is information out there. If we want to be successful, we have to learn these things.

This lecture was very enlightening for me. I had not thought about mediation in this way before. The principles were simple, and we learned many things. This is not an issue that gets solved by one size fits all. If we don't address our problems, the result usually gets worse, and the fire of the conflict becomes hotter. It means that mediation is really a dangerous job. Let's teach and preach this. Mediation has principles and techniques, but sadly we don't know these methods yet. Maybe everything is not that complicated, and we just have to learn it. I understand how much we must work on this issue. Let's learn its different dimensions and prepare those who will play the role of mediator in the Iranian Christian society.

Justice and Forgiveness: I would like to introduce Miroslav Volf, whose books on forgiveness deserve to be translated. He has suffered a lot and his life story is very interesting. He has been subjected to mental and emotional torture. I have read two of his books, *Exclusion and Embrace* and *Free of Charge,* which are very good. However, the book *Exclusion and Embrace* is much more practical, along with theoretical topics. It discusses the Bible verses related to forgiveness.

Matters of mediation can be very problematic. There is a trend where instead of mediation, they are doing something symbolic, justice or truth-telling. In South Africa, Bishop Desmond Tutu and President Mandela, along with the Truth and Reconciliation Commission, emphasised restorative justice. They did not want to destroy the oppressor, but reveal the truth in a public forum.

It seems that the issues of justice and forgiveness, and telling the truth, were not addressed well. Volf in his books, especially in *Free of Charge*, is very clear about how the truth should be expressed. It is not a prescription to simply go and forgive, as if nothing special has happened.

Another issue related to this topic of forgiveness is that, at times, the place of the victim and the offender gets displaced. I find this very harmful to Iranian society. We go to the person who is the victim and tell them to "forgive, forgive, forgive". But the one who has offended the victim is the one who needs to repent of his wrongdoing.

My own experience is that I have been offended a lot. I was not looking for the person who offended me to be punished, but I was looking for the truth to be told. I was the one being blamed, "Why don't you forgive, why don't you forgive?" After a while, I realised that the problem was with the person who had wounded me and not the one who was injured. I feel that, in Iranian society, with the issue of justice versus the revelation of the truth, justice gets sidelined.

Conflicts not Rooted in Truth: Often, our conflicts are not rooted in truth, because we have a different understanding, perspective, and lens from which we approach the situation which has caused the conflict. I completely accept your point that the injustices which are done in many places need to be forgiven. But many times the truth about forgiveness is unclear.

When the problem is looked at from the perspective of both sides, both parties see themselves as being the victim because they have two separate perspectives. It means that, in many instances, the truth is that, from the outside, we can see a problem from the perspective of different people and just try to bring them closer together. This may not happen all the time however. Their understanding of the problem is so strong that they don't want to look at it with a different lens. Your point was very good, and I completely agree that until the truth is known, justice is not served, and forgiveness and healing are unlikely to happen.

The Maturity of the Mediator: Note that we are talking about mediation within the framework of Christianity and the church. Those who are in any kind of leadership in the church are dealing with people. Therefore, willingly or unwillingly, directly or indirectly, they are in relationships. This means that our leaders have a relationship with people, and people have a relationship with them. Also the mediator is in such relationships.

We are talking about mediation within the framework of the church. Whoever wants to work in any kind of ministry, such as disciple-making, is dealing with sinful people who are in relationships. There will always be conflict. Any two people can have different views on issues, different personality types, and different attitudes and future perspectives. When these people get together, the potential for conflict is always there. Conflict is inevitable. There are tensions, separations, and differences in relationships, but the important part is to solve it.

The character of the mediator is very important. The mediator should have reached at least a level of personal maturity in terms of relationships. If the mediator has not reached a level of wisdom and emotional maturity, they can make the problem worse.

Therefore, the personality of the mediator is important. However, we Iranians think we have the abilities and skills to develop good relationships. This assumption rarely opens the door for us to go and learn more abilities and skills. We think we know everything, we are experienced in ministry, so we don't try to learn more. It is not a bad thing to gain further knowledge by learning from each other in seminars like this one.

Breakout Group Report from Reconciliation and Mediation

After the breakout groups, each group was to give a five-minute summary of what their group discussed. The following are summaries of the breakout groups on mediation.

Group 1 – Arabic-speaking (Egyptian, Moroccan, Syrian, Lebanese, Palestinian):
First, we talked about mediation in Egypt. It is easy, since it is a cultural norm outwith the church context, and it helps the church's growth in Egypt. However, it should be noted that the problem is not mediating itself, but choosing the right person for this position. It was also suggested that the mediator should already be a member of the church and have a spiritual position and authority inside the church, as they will then be familiar with the issues in the church and will be wise enough to facilitate the problem.

However, outside Egypt in other Arab communities, it is hard to have this role in the church. This role should be noticed by the leaders of the church as one of the spiritual gifts. The church should have a teacher, a prophet, and a mediator. The church should be aware not to fall into the trap of choosing a mediator who works to appease those in conflict, rather than solving the problem itself.

Another factor in the Arab situation is that you must gain your right or honour back through retaliation, an eye for an eye. So, the mediator's role may not be so easy to do. Self-righteousness is a huge cultural issue within Arab countries, especially when it takes a religious turn. A person may say that he forgives the person but doesn't want any relationship with the offender. So, the mediator should be a trusted wise person and an elderly man. The group had a little disagreement on whether the mediator should be a member of the church or someone from outside the church. The group eventually agreed that if it is a personal issue, the mediator should be known by both parties, but if it is a financial issue, it is fine for the mediator to be a stranger.

Another concern that is the most difficult to mediate is related to marriage, as men may be ashamed to talk about it. The problem must be kept confidential. We discussed that a good solution is to raise the importance of a mediator in dealing with conflict, especially from the BMBs group. We also talked about the problem between fathers and children, especially from BMBs' backgrounds. The familial problems may affect their relationship with God and, in this situation, the mediator may choose not to get all parties involved to discuss this in a better way.

There was a consensus that the role of a mediator is critical. In Egypt, the mediator is easy to be involved in disputes, but in other Arab countries, it is hard to find a mediator.

Group 2

Conflict is a natural feature of our life, and every human being will experience different levels and aspects of it. The first critical issue is the role of a mediator, and we need to equip ourselves with the skills needed for mediation; otherwise, our role as the mediator would intensify the problem and lead to more crises. To educate ourselves, we need to be lifelong learners. As leaders, we must promote mediation skills by holding workshops, translating books, and more specifically, writing and compiling literature for the specific context of the BMBs. We also need trained mediators to address issues that are hard to resolve. However, although we benefit from the social sciences, we should not forget the role of the

Holy Spirit. We must appropriate him and wisely use the gift of the Spirit without ignoring and risking the benefits that social science will have in our mediation.

The second issue is the importance of justice and the revelation of truth. We believe that forgiveness will not happen unless the truth is exposed. Nevertheless, we know that the borders of truth can be blurred in some situations. Still, we must do our best to shed light and uncover the aspects which are clear to enhance the forgiveness process. I would also agree that sometimes coming to a resolution will not be possible. Therefore, we need to have some strategies to deal with situations when the parties in the conflict cannot reconcile. Another important step in conflict resolution is paying attention to the personality of the people concerned. People respond to problems and conflict differently, and their capacities for forgiveness are different. Some are blame shifters and others are avoidant. We discussed that due to the impact of war, many Middle Eastern people have resorted to avoidance, which has made it difficult for them to forgive and reconcile.

Group 3

We had a good conversation and value the recorded messages and the panel discussion. We noticed that it is a strength of the mediator if they are wounded themselves as that allows for more empathy. It was insightful to hear the exposition on Peter who was willing to be corrected by the Apostle Paul. We were wondering if, in the background, Peter being rebuked by Jesus and restored by Jesus was part of his leadership training. Did this lead to him being more humble as a leader and to be a mediator as well?

Our main discussion was about situations in the diaspora. We talked about whether the mediator must be a man. A woman in our group was placed in a situation where she had to mediate and reconcile between two men. As she was successful in that situation, she gained authority. So, mediation can be done by any gender. When you are successful as a mediator, you then gain authority, and people turn to you after that with their problems and seek mediation. This was an encouraging story.

Often the surface conflict is not the immediate reason why there is conflict. There is a long history of trauma and being wounded in their lives and the conflict is only triggered by something they are not able to talk about. Getting to the root cause of the conflict may be a long process. Sadly, we are not often able to touch the real cause.

Our next topic was domestic violence, such as divorce and child protection. In the European/Western setting, it is a 3-step process. You need to talk to the social worker in the case of a marital problem in which divorce is not the immediate solution. If there is physical abuse of children, removing the child from the home may not be the best solution. This needs to be discussed with the social worker or local council. Next, we need to talk to the husband or to the parents in the case of child abuse or neglect. Then we need to talk to the wife and the children. We noticed that women and children are quicker to integrate into the new culture than the men. As mediators, we need to walk alongside the family through the long process of changing behaviours. Initially, there may need to be some compromises, such as talking about patience as they adapt to a new culture. Reconciliation and forgiveness do not necessarily mean that we become best friends afterwards. If we can achieve forgiveness in some situations, it may be best for the parties to go their separate ways.

Lastly, we talked about inter-cultural marriages. It is good for people to realise that when they enter into an inter-cultural marriage, they need to become very skilled in making compromises.

Group 4

We felt that there can be no reconciliation if one of the sides is not interested. It is tougher if both sides are not willing to be brought together to reconcile. It also takes humility on both sides because, through the conflict, they have lost their honour and have been shamed for what has happened. It is tough for them to come to reconciliation unless in some way they preserve their honour in front of people in the right way. Sometimes, it is necessary to go to a professional counsellor. There are individuals who have conflicts that follow them wherever they go. It could be one of the leaders of the church who is fighting with everyone in the church. In this scenario, there is little that a lay leader can do to address the deep problem, so going for professional counselling is the only option in this case.

Another dimension is the individual BMB themselves and the reflection of the context. For some BMBs, their Christian life does not go beyond their testimony. The transformation has not gone beyond their conversion experience, for their lives have not changed. They have the same cultural patterns of interaction as before their conversion. We were laughing in our discussion because it mirrors saying the Shahadah in Islam in which you say something, and you automatically become a Muslim. The Christian presents the gospel and offers a prayer to become a Christian, expecting this prayer to make the person a Christian. Yet, there is no change. Something needs to happen in their lives, so they know what it means to love your enemy and to love your neighbour. If this transformation doesn't happen, then it is difficult to work with this person. They need to let the Holy Spirit work in their heart so they would be open to his working in their lives and reconciling with others with whom they have conflict.

We also discussed a problem in which evangelists are too quick to baptise the new convert without giving them some time to mature in the Lord and in their relationships with their brothers and sisters in the Lord. So, we suggest that the pathway to baptism needs to slow down to make sure that they are growing in their relationship with the Lord and with their neighbours. We agree with the other group that just because we have forgiven and reconciled with the other person, we don't need to be friends. In addition, we need some time for emotions to calm down before we deal with reconciliation. If people are so angry and full of emotional issues, we need to take a pause for things to settle down. It can take a couple of months, or in one case it took two years before the offended parties were ready to address the conflict. The importance of prayer must be stressed with those who are offended. We also talked about the mediator who needs to be accepted by both sides. It can be an insider or outsider, for the key ingredient is the person upon whom they agree to act as a mediator. In some cases, we recognised that the conflict is beyond our control and God will have to intervene in the conflict. We need to be open to this possibility.

Group 5 – Iranian Group

At times, our churches have become places of harm instead of places of reconciliation. We are seeing that our ethnic churches are becoming places that people are trying to avoid after their first encounters, for they have been hurt in one way or another. We have identified six areas that need to be addressed.

1. *Cultural Identity.* We usually internalise the ideas we hear from those around us and that internalisation shapes our identity. It is important to increase our cultural self-esteem by focusing on the positive aspects of cultures as well. We need to identify our culture as Iranian Christians, but it can be extended to Arabic Christians as well, so that others from outside would not have to base their understanding of us based only on the stereotypes they know.
2. *Encouragement in Teaching.* We need to focus both on the positive and negative aspects of our culture. The negative issues that are usually emphasised are pride and the concern about how it will damage the church. However, we also know that our culture has a lot of positive aspects. One of our members was talking about the danger of a single story, which is usually focused on honour and shame as the only aspect of our culture. But our culture is much more complex and has many positive characteristics that we can also talk about as we encourage each other. Mediation is an important element in our culture, and we do that on a daily basis. Mothers are put into a situation where they do that between the fathers and children in the families. Teaching is very important.
3. *Consideration for Reconciliation.* We often focus on reconciling our relationships, but we don't realise how toxic and damaging these relations can be. Both parties can share their hearts partially, but not fully. They usually hide their negative feelings during the process of reconciliation, and therefore, a long-term relationship is not achieved. So that might be something else we need to consider.
4. *Consultation.* The transfer of experience is very important. We are glad that this consultation was organised and it has helped us to gain a lot of wisdom and knowledge from others. We think it should be an ongoing process.
5. *Focus on Forgiveness as an Element of Reconciliation.* Our understanding of forgiveness is very important. Sometimes, co-serving together may not be an option so asking quickly to continue a close relationship is not advised. It is interesting that Luke 17:3 seems to be suggesting that repentance is a condition for forgiveness. If someone is not repentant, why are we forcing ourselves to forgive when the person doesn't want forgiveness? It may be an insult to say "I forgive you" without repentance. Forgiveness takes time. It is important to understand how this relationship

has negatively affected us throughout a time when we see the damages and harm coming out and through us. We must go back through the process of forgiveness. While forgiveness may start as a decision right after the conflict, forgiveness will be ongoing and never end because you are constantly learning how something negatively impacts us.

6. *Apologising is Representative of the Collective Group.* When people are harmed by a group leader or a specific gender, the tendency is to generalise so all ministers or all people of that gender are known as oppressors. A way of confronting the tendency to generalise a group that has harmed another is to become a member of that group, i.e., male, female, or minister. Then apologise as a representative of that collective group. We have seen how that brings healing as well if the person themself will not do it.

Group 6 This group was recorded in full above (pages 73-84).

Group 7

The theory for mediation is correct, but sometimes the mediation is more complex or difficult than we envision. Because of sin, mediation doesn't always work. Sometimes, division or animosity is severe. Sometimes two groups in a church have good hearts and great vision, but they don't reconcile. But, because of sin, there is still separation even if two great churches result because of that division. It takes time to heal after a division or a split. The role of the mediator is not just to bring two people or groups together. Sometimes a conclusion is already made before the mediation is requested. We looked at the splits in the Bible, two in particular. With Paul and Barnabas, the result was two great missionary teams. But it does appear that there was a resolution at the end of Paul's life by accepting John Mark. With Paul and Peter, it could have led to Pauline and Petrine churches, but there was a resolution there. Splits reflect ongoing brokenness in Christ's body, but God redeems our brokenness. By God's grace, some Iranian churches split, and the result is new churches, but the split still reflects sin causing division. A good reason for a church to divide is when a portion of a church is spun off to plant a new church. That should be more prominent than splitting over differences. A positive example was given of a new person coming into a mission and suggesting all sorts of changes. Some leaders suggested that he go off and start his own mission where he could put his ideas into practice. The new man did go off and he started Frontiers, which has planted many churches among Muslims all over the world.

We must unite in prayer to combat our common enemy, Satan, so that we do not become divided or become enemies within our churches. Being united and loving one another is quite different than everyone thinking the same thing. Diversity can be helpful and healthy. The reality is that we are all different, but we should co-operate and not celebrate or encourage division. If we love one another, it is a body working together. If division or splits are caused by sin, God can still redeem the division. Thanks be to God for redeeming our mistakes.

Group 8

We discussed the scriptures that were shared in Matthew 5 and 18. Matthew 5 asks, when I upset someone, what should I do? Matthew 18 says, I'm upset and what should I do? The first step in both of those passages is to go and talk to the other person. While we want to be good mediators, we also need to preach and teach what Jesus said, and see what unfolds from that. Then determine the next step. We also need to keep asking the why question because often the surface issue isn't the deeper issue. As we unpacked that thought, there is often a lot more to it than whatever caused the original conflict. We loved the storytelling and realised the value of sharing reconciliation stories and how helpful and meaningful they are. A story sticks in your mind. We get the best stories when Jesus shares stories throughout the New Testament. It is a good practice to share these stories because they can be very helpful. You can be proactive and inoculate the group you are working with ahead of time by saying from the beginning that there will be conflict. We are human and conflict will be an ongoing thing. If people are forewarned, it won't be such a shock when problems arise. We need to be humble and talk about our own brokenness. We also talked about the biblical concept of lament.

We talked about the language used in dealing with conflict and mediating, which can make a difference. Knowing your audience and the people you are working with is important. It is important to know that if your heart is at war, the problem is with you first. We really appreciated the speakers and felt that they shared a lot of great information.

Conclusion

Although the discussion didn't take the path that was anticipated, which was that mediation is a culturally acceptable model in handling conflict in the North African, Middle Eastern, and Iranian contexts, the discussion reflected the trust established between participants during the consultation. The participants brought out the complex reality of trying to do mediation. They expressed that rarely is mediation simply to determine who has been wronged and what solution can be found to restore the relationship. It is far more complex, requiring great wisdom and insight about situations in which there may be no solution.

For example, if the mediator was a friend of one of the parties in the dispute, the expectation is that the mediator is to side with the friend and not be a neutral arbitrator. In mediation, the parties could be withholding information that only comes out later that should have been disclosed at the beginning. Trauma plays an important part in the conflict and may make reaching an acceptable solution impossible. It will take time, perhaps years, to support a traumatised person before they are ready to forgive others.

A shift took place in the discussion to what is needed are good true stories of what reconciliation and forgiveness look like. Stories are powerful, yet there are few stories that come from this cultural context to give a vision of what the Christian life looks like in putting into place the biblical mandate of Colossians 3:12-14, "Therefore, as God's chosen people, holy and dearly loved, clothe yourselves with compassion, kindness, humility, gentleness, and patience. Bear with each other and forgive one another if any of you has a grievance against someone. Forgive as the Lord forgave you. And over all these virtues put on love, which binds them all together in perfect unity."

7: A Way Forward:
Turning the Upside-Down Right Side Up

Conflict is the reality that the human race has lived with since the Fall and is a part of the curse of humankind's disobedience of eating the fruit from the forbidden tree of the knowledge of good and evil (Gen. 2:15-17). Although conflict has similar expressions in various cultures, there are cultural expressions that are uniquely shaped in each society. The purpose of bringing together leaders from a Muslim background from three geographic regions, which are Muslim majority, is to provide a safe place for sharing and reflection where church leaders can honestly share their experiences with peers without judgement and explore insights from an intercultural perspective, drawing on the wisdom each community has learned and experienced. It was a unique opportunity for BMB leaders to be self-examined, analyse their heritage and reconsider the roots of the problems that they face today which result from their heritage. BMBs, like the rest of the global church, need to see the world through Christ's lens and filter what we should embrace and what should be redeemed in our culture.

Our main goal in this chapter is to address how to interpret our communities in light of Christ and how to move these communities experiencing conflict, particularly with the first generation who have come out of Islam, to a pathway of hope for the church's future. In order to do that, we recognise that the goal of discipleship is transformation, not just survival in a hostile environment. Simply put, the transformation of the individual is to become more like Christ. As stated in the introduction, discipleship will take a lifetime with the intention to transform the behaviour, beliefs, and worldviews, not only of the individual, but also of the nascent church community.

Often, leaders of small house fellowships are chosen because they may have a charismatic personality, are gifted evangelists, or are gifted teachers. Sometimes, these leaders are put into leadership positions by necessity without enough examination of their character or how mature they are as Christian leaders, which was discussed earlier. If we desire to see a real transformation, the worldview that forms the cultural tendencies must be addressed at its root. This is not an easy task. Most people assume that the cultural worldview they have been raised in is how things are to be done; changing it will meet resistance, both by BMBs and the broader community. Yet, Jesus challenged the prevailing worldview of his time calling for his new disciples to stop the cycle of conflict, retribution, anger, and other sinful behaviour. Jesus calls his believers to a higher standard and confronts sacredly held cultural values and behaviours. This is seen in the Sermon on the Mount when he says, "You have heard that it was said to the people long ago [...]. But I tell you [...]" (Mt. 5-6).

The consultation from which this book comes was a platform for acknowledgement and positive criticism. It was a safe place to highlight communication challenges that BMBs experience, which is a challenge for all Christian believers. However, there are nonetheless some specific challenges due to the legal and social status of the BMB.

The Christian background community in the MENA region is challenged by similar challenges that BMBs experience in terms of communication, leadership, and conflict resolution issues. The change we long to see should include the broader church community, not only BMBs. Jesus was culturally a Middle Easterner and spoke to both the sinful nature and cultural tendencies of his time. At the same time, he was considered a rebel by the greater community, as his teachings and deeds challenged deeply held customs and power structures dictating behaviour, as he called people into the Kingdom of God. Jesus is calling his believers to a higher standard, to be a city on a hill that is the light of the world. "A town built on a hill cannot be hidden" (Mt. 5:14-16). This happens through asking the right questions and viewing the church through the eyes of Jesus our Lord.

There is a cost in stopping the cycle of one's behaviour – their own culture; for some, it is too costly. Jesus is calling us to embrace the cost in a continuous pattern of behavioural change, that becomes a new culture itself (Mt. 16:24-26). This new way of living will be resisted by the wider community. Paul informs Timothy that there will be persecution, "Everyone who wants to live a godly life in Christ Jesus will be persecuted" (2 Tim. 3:12). This new community, trying to live out being conformed to the image of Christ, will, by its nature, expose the sinful behaviour, beliefs, and worldviews of others and that will be resisted by family, community, and power structures of religions. Yet the living body of Christ, the church, is to be a countercultural change agent of the Kingdom of God. The nascent church needs to be clear that it is a community of people who live out the Gospel. Although it is hard, it will move us from conflict to hope.

In order to create an environment which will be able to sustain the new community, three ingredients need to be put into the DNA of the new Christian and the new church fellowship. These three are trust, vulnerability, and accountability. For the church to grow in maturity, stable core groups need to be formed who help build mature Christians. Discipleship done on a one-to-one basis does not have the impact of modelling a community of trust to people who have experienced broken trust on multiple levels. Therefore, discipleship is most effective when done in community. Establishing a good community based on the three principles of trust, vulnerability, and accountability is best done in small groups. The small group context provides a community of trust small enough that we can remove our masks to share what is happening in our private lives and thoughts. This group of trusted individuals can help us along our spiritual journey since they will know the areas we struggle in and understand the season of life we are in.

This consultation is an example of building a community of trust, as we discussed issues that are *haram* or forbidden to talk about. We created a safe place to discuss conflict, which is like cancer invading the body of Christ. If we avoided discussing the four areas of conflict, it would have serious ramifications for the church. In this last chapter, we will explore how to transform the pull of the prevailing culture to pull with new values that will bring hope to the church fellowships struggling with conflict. The church lives in an upside-down world. Jesus came to redeem a world lost in sin and turn this world right side up as God created it to be. We live in a redemptive community that is here but not yet, meaning we will always struggle with sin and cultural tendencies, but we also have the example of Christ, the Word of God, and the power of the Holy Spirit to guide and direct us in the way that we should live. We are a living story; by confronting our cultural tendencies in small groups, we can create a pathway to healing and health in our churches.

This chapter is written by the authors based on the presentations and discussions that took place.

Pathway Toward Healing and Hope: Communication

Identification of the Problem

Miscommunication is a major problem in every culture. Every person and culture comes with their own perspective on communication. For instance, people from different cultures communicate differently. Some tend toward direct communication, not being afraid of conflict, while others use indirect communication, avoiding tension or conflict. Even something as simple as greeting someone can carry different messages. For example, shaking hands carries a message of trust or equality, kisses on the cheek carries a message of friendship, and bowing carries a message of showing honour to the other. But even in each example of greeting are variations and complexities that could be fuel for conflict. The potential for miscommunication is ever present on every level of society. Ever since the Fall in Genesis 3, communication has been a problem in our vertical communication with God and horizontally between people. The Bible is full of examples of the conflict and the destruction that communication confusion can bring.

To move from conflict to hope, we need to identify some of the complexities of the problem. If we just go to the Bible and preach passages that deal with communication, we are missing important steps that were presented in the introduction. We must become self-aware that personal and cultural patterns of communication are part of the problem. Biblical exegesis of the scripture will expose our patterns of communication and good preaching/teaching should create the hermeneutical bridge which moves people between the biblical culture to their own. Critical contextualisation takes into consideration the religious, national, and cultural perspectives and points to the hope we have in living in a new community. This book explores the cultural reality that is influencing the church with this last chapter paving a new way to give hope to the burgeoning new church.

Explanation of the Complexities of Communication

As was discussed in the introduction, North Africa, the Middle East, and Iran score high on power distance. This cultural value affects communication in a hierarchical order. People in leadership hold the power and influence, so the leader expects to be unchallenged in their opinions. Subordinates are expected to be told what to do. This means that the role models people have grown up with may not have the knowledge base and experience of someone growing up in a low power distant culture where communication is based on equality. In the same way, these countries score very high on uncertainty avoidance. Uncertainty avoidance means the acceptable cultural way of communicating is to use indirect communication. Therefore, true intentions are not verbally expressed, because these may cause tension or conflict. People feel compelled to be polite to avoid hurting someone's self-esteem. Truth-telling can seem very scary and is avoided at any cost. To avoid possible conflict, people will talk around the subject, expecting the other to discover what is being actually said.

These patterns of communication can cause frustration for the pastor trying to lead the church. The pastor could ask the elders in private what they think about certain decisions and the direction of the church, but when it comes to stating their perspective publicly in a meeting, these same elders might say what they think the congregation is thinking, to not go against the perceived opinion of the congregation. Or the pastor could hold to an egalitarian perspective of shared leadership with the elders, but the elders believe that the position stated in the meeting was only a whisper to express what the pastor thinks the elders want. In private, the elders still believe that the pastor is the boss (high power distance) and does not want to share leadership.

This model of hierarchy in leadership is accepted culturally in the Iranian, Middle Eastern and North African contexts. Culturally, the Pastor / Priest is God's representative for the congregation. He is the channel for God's voice, but people can be so indoctrinated by how leaders regularly say one thing in private and another thing in public that people generally do not trust what leaders say. The pastor has a large influence on his congregation. Pastors with strong personalities and hierarchical leadership have the last say in every matter related to their congregation. For example, they use the pulpit to preach about the problem and interpret the solution. The pulpit has a great authority in our religious communities, which is a double-edged sword. The pastor might come from the feeling of honour and love, but sometimes it leads to conflict, lack of freedom of expression, and oppression.

Another dimension that complicates communication is when someone links their identity to their opinion or point of view. It creates a zero-sum view of the conflict, where one's very existence seems inextricably linked to the negation of the other. To give in to someone's opinion or perspective is viewed as questioning one's own authority. Their beliefs are so rigid that they are extremely resistant to change, which results in closing down any ability to communicate. A word picture is of two individuals, male or female, standing face-to-face, yelling their point of view without listening to what the other person is saying.

Communication can be stunted when an individual or group has a very limited understanding of a subject or are new Christians. Bringing in other perspectives can be viewed as a personal attack on the faith which they have come to accept. New believers who have a limited understanding of the scripture may consider introducing alternative theological understanding, such as an Arminian argument to a staunch Calvinist, would be viewed as changing the gospel.[11] These are just a few examples of the complexities that lead to conflict in communication. Hope will come when obstacles to good communication are discussed and confronted to bring healing and hope to the church. We would encourage each fellowship or church to develop its own list of communication challenges and talk about them in small groups.

The Church Can Stand in the Gap to Stop the Cycle of Conflict

Moving forward, one of the issues that needs to be addressed is the fear of miscommunicating. In particular, the first generation has been so influenced by cultural ways of communicating that it is considered normal for people to hide their true feelings and opinions. The understood correct way to talk to someone is to honour the person through praise and deflection in communication. Saying what you really mean would seem offensive and impolite.

Steps forward to healing and hope must include establishing trust which needs to be a high priority. As discussed in the previous chapters, there are three ingredients which are necessary to establish healthy communication. One way is to establish small groups which have the purpose of building a community of trust, vulnerability, and accountability. In order to do that, there needs to be a safe place where forbidden subjects can be openly discussed. In these small groups, the purpose is to establish new perspectives, values, goals, and boundaries that comprise the godly life. There are two types of small groups – open groups and closed groups. An open group allows anyone to attend. A closed group consists of individuals who are committed to each other and to the rules of the group. The closed group will have only a few people and visitors will not be allowed to attend. This allows the group to establish trust, vulnerability, and accountability. They will need to establish strict rules that everyone in each small group must follow to make sure that what is discussed is not fodder for gossip. Topics discussed in the small group must remain in the small group.

In addition, the nascent church will need to wrestle with biblical passages that discuss a new way of understanding vulnerability in their cultural context. Most fear that people will use the information discussed openly in the small group as material for gossip. Vulnerability is an emotional risk; for instance, in the Middle East, there is a saying "men don't cry". It is a sign of weakness, and sometimes vulnerability becomes a source of shame, exposure, and uncertainty to the consequences of opening up.

We are not talking about being vulnerable with secrets in a worship service where it is naïvely assumed that the Christian community is a safe community.

---

[11] Strict Calvinists believe God is 100% sovereign and he knows everything that will happen because he planned it. Arminians believe God is sovereign, but has limited his control in relation to man's freedom and their response to it.

There must be a strict rule of confidentiality. There can be no violations of this rule. Most people view vulnerability as a weakness. The place to begin is with the leadership team. It is within this small group where trust is established that the potential of setting a new tone in the whole church lies. The more that trust is established, the more comfortable we are to open up and be vulnerable. Vulnerability does not happen immediately. We must have patience and draw others out. There will be some who will watch and see how the others react to open and honest sharing. If there is any perceived judgement or hint of using information against someone in the group, they will typically not open up. That is why Jesus said,

> Do not judge, or you too will be judged. For in the same way you judge others, you will be judged, and with the measure you use, it will be measured to you. Why do you look at the speck of sawdust in your brother's eye and pay no attention to the plank in your own eye? How can you say to your brother, 'Let me take the speck out of your eye,' when all the time there is a plank in your own eye? You hypocrite, first take the plank out of your own eye, and then you will see clearly to remove the speck from your brother's eye. Do not give dogs what is sacred; do not throw your pearls to pigs. If you do, they may trample them under their feet, and turn and tear you to pieces (Mt. 7:1-6).

Passages that present a new way of communicating may include, but are not limited to, passages such as Matthew 5:37, when Jesus tells the people to say simply yes or no, because anything beyond this comes from the evil one. We desire to avoid the condemnation of God in Isaiah 29:13, where people honour God with their lips but their hearts are far from him. We are not to be people described in Psalm 12:2, "Everyone lies to their neighbour; they flatter with their lips but harbour deception in their hearts"; or Proverbs 26:24, "Enemies disguise themselves with their lips, but in their hearts, they harbour deceit." Passages on gossip should also be discussed, such as Proverbs 11:13, 16:28, 18:8, 20:19, 26:20.

Lastly, the small group will be recommended to talk about what accountability will look like in their context. This will seem counter-cultural, but it is in the core of Christ-culture. Jesus held his disciples accountable. Until Christians realise that their lives are in desperate need of help, they will shy away from any sense of accountability. This is particularly true for pastors and other leaders who try to maintain their reputation and the respect of others, while all the while their lives are out of control, their quiet time with God is uninspiring, and their prayer time is non-existent. Spiritual pride keeps many Christians from experiencing the joy and freedom found in Christ and is a wall used to protect their desired reputation.

The hope is to activate accountability as a core practice; however living in the Middle East, North Africa, or Iranian context as a wider community will make it a real challenge for practicing accountability. I can see how hard it is to be applied in a context that generally resists this principle. Most governments in the region refuse to be accountable to their people. The politicians prefer to take credit for positive achievements but avoid admitting their responsibility for the failures. So, the turning point is between what is heavenly and what is earthly. Here, our behaviour should reflect our true identity. Unlike the nature of the fallen world that we live in, the church should be the light for its society also it should reflect the challenges that the society passes through. Accountability is a biblical principle and the church should follow it by default but, when living in a corrupted society, the reflective practice of accountability may vary from one individual to another. There is a price to be paid in order to see the positive change which we hope for. We as BMB leaders have to pay this price in order to see the change. We are not only called to swim against the current in our societies but we are also called to swim against the current inside our church communities.

The Bible has a lot of teaching about accountability. As was discussed in Chapter 4, Iranian culture desires Nathans who encourage others, but not Nathans who hold leaders accountable. However, we have passages, like 2 Samuel 12, that give us the example of Nathan rebuking King David for murder and adultery. Jesus gives a teaching on accountability in Matthew 18:15-20, dealing with someone who sins against you. There are direct passages when Jesus rebukes the disciples for calling down fire on the Samaritan town. The group must come up with rules that everyone can agree upon to be accountable to each other. The ability to hold someone accountable is the test of trust.

It is a complex principle as many other factors affect accountability, such as our heritage, pride and the lack of role models. It is rare to see a leader in our context admit that they have done something wrong. The apology culture is not very active. It is also important to know that Nathan is not well-received in our culture because of the shame / honour and hierarchy.

The Cost of Changing Communication Patterns

There is always a cost when someone or a church decides to go against deeply held cultural patterns of communication. In this matter, a new BMB Christian is entering uncharted territory. The prevailing opinion may be that when anyone ventures outside the prescribed ways of communicating, they are viewed as bringing chaos not only to themselves but to the community. They may be afraid of how they will be viewed by family and friends should they change the way they communicate. Open and honest discussions about the goal of creating a community of trust through a new Christian pattern of communicating should be juxtaposed to the alternative of continuing to live with masks and saying only what the other person wants to hear.

In the mosque community, the religious figure is considered holy and far from being accountable to their congregation, but the congregation are accountable to them. This is similar to the historical church arrangements in the region, to which the majority of the Christians in the Middle East belong. The Middle Eastern model of Christian leadership looks similar to the Islamic leadership. Culturally, the change which leads people to take off their masks and speak their opinion usually comes from the top to the bottom. This initiative should come from the leader/pastor themself to replace the social culture with the biblical culture that includes honesty and a safe place of trust. Also, there is a cost to be paid as a result of this initiative, since leaders can, and on occasions will, be replaced. This is counter-cultural for those of us in the Middle East.

The Role of the Global Church

Changing the way communication is done is too daunting for a local church to undertake on its own. The global church is a great resource for new BMB churches and fellowships. Their support and teaching can encourage the local church and tell them that they are fully supported in addressing longstanding cultural patterns of communication. Christians have wrestled with communication issues in every generation. Although the teachings may be more tailored to a North American or European context, the principles can be applied to every culture when critical contextualisation is implemented. The BMB church is not alone. The new BMB churches can draw upon the lessons learned by the greater body of Christ. Remember that:

"Christ himself gave the apostles, the prophets, the evangelists, the pastors and teachers, to equip his people for works of service, so that the body of Christ may be built up until we all reach unity in the faith and in the knowledge of the Son of God and become mature, attaining to the whole measure of the fullness of Christ" (Eph. 4:11-13).

Honour and Shame

Identification of the Problem

There are many cultures besides the ones mentioned in this resource which are honour/shame cultures. Honour and the preservation of honour are inescapable driving forces in these cultures. The honour of the family is dependent upon conforming to the standards lived out by family, clan, locality, culture, and religion. Shame is used to manipulate others; it is described as causing a heavy feeling of not measuring up to the established cultural standard. Shame carries with it the feeling of being unworthy, unacceptable, and naked. Middle Eastern shame was expressed as burdensome baggage from birth and is inescapable, so it is lifelong. The word picture which was used in Chapter 2 shows that honour and shame are what individuals in these cultures are marinated in.

Explanation of the Complexities of Shame

Honour and shame permeates every facet of life and influences how people interact with each other. For instance, communication is shaped by honour and shame. Direct communication is considered shameful, so the default setting is to use indirect communication. This leaves the other person guessing what the person is trying to communicate, creating a two-fold reality, of what the person said and what is really going on that is hidden. Communication is shaped by honour, so it is beneficial to heap praise on those in leadership. Yet it can also become a pretext to reap the benefit praise might bring, so it might not be genuine. Honour is to be guarded, so transparency is avoided; presenting a good image is important to maintain. Something as banal as asking for directions from someone who doesn't know the answer may result in that person feeling obligated to give any answer just to save face. It is shameful for someone to admit that they don't know the answer.

The complexities do not stop there. For instance, a person is shamed for not living up to familial or cultural standards. On the other hand, a shamed person is more likely to blame others, for admitting weakness is shameful, particularly for a leader of a ministry. This leads to a lack of transparency. A lack of transparency leads to a lack of trust. The domino effect is a lack of forgiveness, a culture of lying and cheating, and the use of flattery and gift-giving to present an honourable image in public. In extreme cases, shaming leaves deep wounds, resulting in hypersensitivity to anything that might be perceived as a personal attack or further shaming. This creates tension in the fellowship; left unaddressed, it will create instability in the fellowship.

Richard and Evelyn Hibbert, who had worked in Bulgaria in the 1990s, researched why people had defected from their local churches. First, they discovered that everyone still affirmed their faith in Christ. Second, they didn't feel accepted in the churches because of gossiping, people taking offense and holding grudges, and being unable to humble themselves to ask for forgiveness. The last ingredient was poor leadership (Lidstone, 2019: 9-11). Lidstone documents that a similar situation played out among the Muslim Uyghurs in the 1990s living in eastern Kazakhstan. The same poor community formation and poor leadership were the fundamental problems.

Honour and shame greatly influence leaders of fellowships and churches. It is honourable to be a leader, which the scriptures encourage us to be (1 Tim. 3:1). On the other hand, those suffering from feelings of being unworthy, unacceptable, and naked will desire to be someone with honour and respect in the fellowship, hiding their insecurities. There can be a constant desire to be the leader of the church or to stand before others, regardless of qualifications, for there is an intrinsic desire to have people think highly of the individual.

Honour and shame will also impact the process of mediation. An honourable person would not become totally transparent when confronted, for the focus is to compare oneself with others. Private matters must remain private. The cost of losing face with others is too high of a cost. Those called upon to mediate shared frustration at the lack of transparency needed to go to the root problem.

The church community shares in the blame. It is cultural to desire to have a hero or saviour, so they will impost that upon the pastor or church leader. Such pressure put on the leadership is more than someone can bear. It creates the need for the hero leader, at least on the surface, to live up to the expectations of being a leader or they will lose face in the eyes of the church fellowship. The church does not want a servant leader, for that would be shameful.

Shame and Expectations

Another layer of shame comes from Islam, which has institutionalised shame upon non-Muslims. For those becoming Christ followers, this stigma follows them throughout their lives. It becomes more complex because shame works both ways, the status of *murtadd*, the most shameful term for a convert, is projected upon the family, community, nation, and religion. The intensity of this shame depends on the family or community. The more conservative they are, the greater impact the shame will bear on the family or community. Shame in this specific case is legitimate because when a BMB proclaims that they are no longer a Muslim, that is considered a rejection from their side, to dishonour their family, heritage, community and sometimes their nationality. The shame in this case is considered as failing the trust. It is for this reason that many fellowships should be discrete and underground to avoid drawing the attention and being noticed by their community. We recommend each BMB fellowship community to come up with their own challenges list of honour/shame relevant to their specific context. It is highly important to identify these challenges and address them practically and come up with tangible practical set of actions that teach our BMB communities how to reflect Christ's values within our shame culture. It is important to know the roots of shame in every situation we have and address them with love as Jesus did. Christ was in a position of shame from his own community on so many occasions and he always responded to that with positive attitude and asking the right questions.

The Church Can Stand in the Gap to Stop the Cycle of Conflict

The first step in moving to hope is to recognise that the first generation is the one who will suffer most from what was called Post Traumatic Shame Disorder (PTSD) and the baggage that comes with it. Much of the time discipling new believers will be spent on creating stability since there is so much dishonour associated with conversion. In addition, the new convert will likely have reactions of self-pity, victimisation, or fear. The global church can help by providing excellent teaching and resources to both understand what is happening and provide tools to help the nascent church through this period of stabilisation.

Second, the church needs to preach and teach that it is honourable to suffer loss and make sacrifices in coming to Christ. The church needs to teach BMBs to expect suffering but not to seek suffering as happens in some cases. Christ taught much on suffering for the sake of the gospel (the Beatitudes, Mt. 5:3-12; witnessing, Mt. 10). The New Testament church encouraged one another to enter into the sufferings of Christ (Rom. 8:17-20; 2 Cor. 1:3-11; Phil. 3:7-10; 1 Tim. 1:8-12). Christ is to be the focus; he covers our shame (Rom. 10:11). The Bible is written in a culture steeped in honour and shame, with stories, illustrations, and teachings from this perspective. Western culture misses this unique point of view; the Middle Eastern church has much to teach the Western church about reading scripture through Middle Eastern eyes as Jesus himself was Middle Eastern who spoke to his community who have many similarities to the current communities.

Third, the church and mission agencies should have a long-term perspective, understanding that it will take several generations to develop a good theology and practice of living biblically in a shame culture. As the nascent church builds upon the successes and failures of dealing with the wounds many carry from being shamed, it will develop a contextual theology and practice. As new converts understand and reorient their perspective built on a redemptive countercultural community that builds each other up instead of tearing each other down, it will stabilise.

Fourth, it is important to develop into the DNA of the new believer and churches that transparency is not shameful, but it is an important practice in the Christian life. This does not mean openly speaking about infidelities in a church service. Instead, a structure should be put into place within the fellowship, so all are kept accountable. A culture of humility, transparency, and admission of failures needs to be a core value from the beginning of discipleship. The pastor/leader and elders also need to develop this culture in their own life and ministry. It should not be shameful to admit that all have sinned. This new culture should extend beyond the local setting, for leaders and influencers in the Middle East need to model that all are under the authority and in submission to the global church. Leaders need to model how they receive correction and openly talk about how they have to be corrected without shame. It is important from the leaders as role models to admit failures so their congregations have realistic expectations from themselves and not to have delusions and false expectations from their Christian lives. There is a false expectation that life as a Christian means that we sin no more and our leaders are God – they cannot do anything wrong. This misconception needs to be corrected and the change must happen from the top down.

The Role of the Global Church

The global church has done a lot of research and teaching on Post Traumatic Stress Disorder (PTSD). It is beneficial for the global church to provide an understanding of the phenomena of PTSD, its diagnosis, and treatment. Those suffering from the shame that comes from abuse, whether it be psychological, physical, sexual, financial, or emotional abuse are likely to be suffering from some form of PTSD. Unless abuse is stopped, it will continue for generations, because those who are abused tend to abuse others.

Leadership

Identification of the Problem

The default setting in the Middle Eastern, North African, and Iranian contexts is the desire for strong authoritarian leaders who can take control of the church and tell the congregation what to do and think. This is normative in hierarchical cultures. Servant leadership is a rarity and often misunderstood as a weakness. The situation is made more acute because there is not enough time to cultivate and mentor new emerging leaders after Christ's servant model. It takes years of teaching and mentoring, which these new churches do not have. The pressing need is for someone to lead the emerging church now. Those gifted or who show potential for leadership are put into leadership positions without allowing for time or consideration of the character needed to be a biblical leader of a congregation. When conflict arises, the leadership model they have grown up with becomes the default response, leading to toxic and abusive leadership. Toxic leadership creates fear within the fellowship, so compliance with the leader, splitting the church, or leaving becomes the experience in BMB churches.

Julyan Lidstone identifies twelve symptoms of toxic patron leadership (Lidstone, 2019: 12-17):

1. Toxic leaders use their authority in a domineering and controlling way
2. Toxic leaders expect to be consulted about minor matters
3. Toxic leaders are poor at delegation
4. Toxic leaders silence the truth by suppressing criticism
5. Toxic leaders discipline by shunning and exclusion
6. Toxic leaders compete with and criticise other leaders and other churches
7. Toxic leaders view emerging leaders as a threat
8. Toxic leaders cannot admit to weakness
9. Toxic leaders avoid transparency and accountability
10. Toxic leaders cling to leadership roles
11. Toxic leaders seek to accumulate the perks of office
12. Toxic leaders burn out on conflict and emotional pressures.

Explanation of the Complexities of Toxic Leaders

The cultural role model of a leader is to be a strong authoritarian leader or a benevolent autocrat. The benevolent autocrat is to take care of those under his/her/their care, creating patron/client relationships. The layers of complexity are like the layers of an onion. Leaders think that the general public cannot handle the truth. An Arab proverb states, "When a blind man can see with one eye, it is better than not being able to see at all." Therefore, the pastor or leader makes statements concerning the church in public, but in private, they may think or act differently.

First, the cultural pull of power distance means we can expect the ideal pastor to be a benevolent autocrat, which is good. However, due to our sinful nature, church leaders become less than ideal; they can become toxic, and controlling leaders. Toxic leaders create an atmosphere of fear in their all-controlling dominance. To maintain their authority, pastors tend to become aloof, not ministering to the needs of the congregation. Since all the authority resides in the pastor, they make unilateral decisions. This is complicated by communication styles where members defer to the leader even when they disagree. The toxicity is further complicated by shaming members from the pulpit, and even repeating things said in confidence. To keep control of the congregation, toxic pastors will resort to criticising other pastors and churches.

Second, the expectation in a hierarchical society is for congregation be told what to do. With our sinful tendencies, members become compliant, deferring to the will of the pastor. They also expect the pastor to benefit the members, who in exchange give their loyalty. The congregation looks for a hero to lead the people and to have a strong personality.

The third source of fuelling toxicity comes from the outside. The pastor is expected to have more benefits given to them, which can lead to justification to solicit more money from external sources, which will eventually lead to conflict in the church. Mission agencies seeking to benefit the struggling church extend gifts of money, equipment, and services, which feeds into the patron mentality with the role of the pastor as the benefactor.

Lastly, the isolation of leaders from the broader Christian community is a problem. Most churches of BMBs are independent with no ecclesiastical structure in place for accountability and fellowship. Isolation creates an environment where the leader is not accountable to nor transparent with anyone. Rarely are there the checks and balances in place which are essential in ministry. The reason for the lack of oversight is: first, most churches are small and new, and do not have mature believers who could play this role. Second, the culture will accept supportive Jonathans, but these churches are not mature enough to accept mentoring that includes corrective criticism. Nathans who challenge leaders even discreetly are rarely accepted. Third, fellowships are independent by necessity, operating below the radar of governmental or religious leaders, so as not to call attention to the new community.

As it was so clearly stated in the discussion groups, trying to change the structure and expectations is a no-win scenario. Chinchen gives a possible way to redeem the structure of a strong authoritarian leader or a benevolent autocrat.

Corrupt Patronage	**Redeemed Patronage**
Starts with client making a large demand	Starts with client making a small gift of appreciation
False hopes, false securities, intentional creation of fictitious insecurities	Truth, honesty, openness, integrity, promises fulfilled
Weak, self-serving relationships	Strong, authentic relationships
Utilitarian and materialistic	Genuine and sincere
Proud patron insists on titles and status	Humble patron honours the client
Proud and unwilling to visit the client	Visits and nurtures the client
Proud patron, above questioning	Humble patron, who can admit faults
Insists on balanced reciprocity	Unconditional, self-sacrificing love
Possessive, keeps client inferior	Aims for client's maturity and independence

Table from Chinchen, 1995: 446-451

The Church Can Stand in the Gap to Stop the Cycle of Conflict

Hope will come when we teach and talk about toxic leadership in the church. This includes discussing the atmosphere of fear, aloofness that does not minister to the needs of the congregation, and the propensity to make unilateral decisions. The second step is to put in place a system of accountability with senior leadership in the country or region. No pastor or house fellowship should work independently of some structural oversight. This can be difficult in certain closed countries where security is a big issue due to persecution, but it should not be used as an excuse for those in leadership to act independently.

There are two important benefits for pastors or leaders of house churches who have leadership oversight. The first benefit addresses burnout that can happen with isolated leaders who carry the burdens of their church alone. Fellowship with senior leaders in the country can provide needed encouragement. This fellowship will allow the country leader to hear and see if the pastor is overburdened and prevent potential burnout. The second benefit is mentoring, which includes two dimensions. The first is that mentoring house church leaders is like on-the-job training to gain better skills in being a leader. The second dimension includes addressing problem areas. The relationship between the mentor and mentee must be built upon trust to the point where there is vulnerability. In Chapter 4, it was proposed that servant leadership needs to be taught to the extent that no leader can say, "I don't need others to counsel me."

The members of the church need someone they can appeal to when there is a conflict with the leader. Members have often left because of toxic leadership. But leaving should not be the only option. The congregation should also know that there is someone to whom the leader is responsible. When problems occur in the church, they should know that there is someone with whom they can raise their concerns.

The Cost of Stopping Toxic Leaders

There is resistance in going against the prevailing patterns that are so culturally ingrained in society. The struggle is establishing an accountability structure that can address the toxic leader. For the insecure pastor, there is fear in trusting someone besides themselves. The cost will be different for each person, but this is where the mentor can help the mentee to understand the cost as Jesus said, "Whoever wants to be my disciple must deny themselves and take up their cross daily and follow me" (Lk. 9:23).

The Role of the Global Church

The global church is a great resource for new BMB churches and fellowships to draw upon. Christians have wrestled with toxic leadership in every culture and every generation. Although the teachings may be more tailored to a particular context, like Western churches, the principles used can be applied to every culture when critical contextualisation is included. The BMB church need not struggle alone when it comes to training leaders.

1. The global church can show the way for humble, vulnerable, authentic, and healthy mission agencies, as exemplified in their relationships and churches' ministries, to come alongside the emerging leadership of the BMB church.

2. In order to prevent the problem of putting toxic leaders in positions of authority, we need a comprehensive view of leadership, which starts with discipleship from the very beginning of the Christian life.
3. Leaders need to create a mentoring culture of learning by modelling it well with emerging leaders.
4. The panel discussion suggested creating structures of accountability, instead of each church or fellowship being an island unto itself. It is important to have ecclesiastical structures to oversee the mentorship, training, and accountability of the emerging leadership of house churches in the North African, Middle Eastern, and Iranian contexts.

Mediation

Identification of the Problem

Each culture has its challenges in addressing conflict. Great wisdom is needed in any situation in which mediation is required. Mediation in the three regions that this study focuses on has been expressed as complicated and very painful. In a shame/honour culture, there are many cultural layers that need to be considered. Mediation has a long history in the worldwide Muslim community and is steeped in Islamic traditions which also need to be considered. For instance, BMBs joining the Christian community brings the assumption that this Christian community is the real definition of what real *ummah* should look like. The perspective is that my brother is responsible for me and I am responsible for my brother. When the new Christian community is found to have problems, BMBs can get discouraged and leave the fellowship.

Mediation imported from another culture will need to be adapted to the cultural context. To fully understand mediation, the mediator and the parties offended all have perspectives which must be considered. Each person brings their own failures, familial backgrounds on how conflict is addressed or avoided, and communication patterns that must be understood in the mediation process. The emotional maturity of the people in the dispute can influence and significantly complicate the process of mediation. We know that mediation works when the offended parties stop the hostility. The goal is conflict resolution and not just conflict management. Conflict management is to minimise dysfunctional conflict and maximise functional or constructive conflict. Conflict resolution is to reduce, terminate, or eliminate the conflict. The ideal is to restore the relationship between the two parties. Communication is such a large component in mediation and is multi-layered, needing wisdom from God.

Explanation of the Complexities of Mediation

Mediation is never a simple process for there are cultural understandings of how mediation works, and also the personal baggage which each person brings into the conflict.

First, there are cultural, familial, and religious triggers which can upset people. These can be perceived as insults, lack of respect, and shaming. Shame and honour play a large role in seeking mediation, for admitting pain makes people feel ashamed. The emphasis on honour may create a perception that admitting a problem destroys the reputation of the person, especially if they hold a leadership position in the church. Since these cultures are very expressive, conflicts can flare up very quickly and passionately and the emotions may be too raw to seek mediation.

Second, individuals involved in the conflict can take a zero-sum attitude, in which everything is seen as being at stake in the outcome of the conflict and one's identity is directly tied to it. This is expressed as an all-or-nothing approach to conflict. Rarely is it an issue of one person being right and the other wrong.

Third, the expectation people have of the mediator can complicate things. If the mediator is a friend of both sides in the conflict, it is assumed that the mediator will take the side of a friend. Neutrality of the mediator may not be the expectation. Most of the time, the mediator becomes part of the conflict itself, especially in the eyes of the losing party.

Fourth is the role that trauma plays in conflict. The mediator will need to understand how trauma has impacted the conflict to be addressed. Trauma can prevent forgiveness and reconciliation. The mediator needs to be sensitive to the complexity of the shame culture while admitting the trauma and trying to find a common ground where they can address the conflict.

Fifth concerns the collective memory of a society. If there are a lack of stories of how mediation has happened in real-life cases, people may not understand that forgiveness and reconciliation are possible. It is important for every BMB community to recognise the act of mediation when it happens and share the story within their congregation and praise this act of mediation so it becomes a clear core value for the community.

Sixth, when mediating conflicts in marriage, mostly men and sometimes women may be ashamed to talk about their problems – according to their culture, what happens in the house should remain in the house. There is a tension when marital conflicts become obvious and need mediation. It needs a big step of trust to share which magnifies the responsibility on the mediator. Intercultural marriages bring with them a package of different worldviews and may seem irreconcilable or hard to work with. Mediation in this case plays a vital role for preparation for counselling and helps in redeeming broken relationships.

Seventh, mediation affecting an entire church could be over theological perspectives or traditions, or over approaches to leadership. As one of the presenters said, "Mediators accept their role in our communities, even though it sometimes is a very difficult responsibility to accept." But eventually, it is known how vital and important, and how in some contexts mediation is considered a cultural obligation.

The Church Can Stand in the Gap to Stop the Cycle of Conflict

Hope comes when the church has a role to play in mediation. Each church should understand that conflict is inevitable. The church should teach about mediation, for Paul admonishes, "Brothers and sisters, if someone is caught in a sin, you who live by the Spirit should restore that person gently. But watch yourselves, or you also may be tempted. Carry each other's burdens, and in this way you will fulfil the law of Christ" (Gal. 6:1-2). If there is no one in the small house church or fellowship who has the characteristics of a mediator, they should connect with someone in the region who can be called upon as a Christian mediator. Cultivating a community of trust, vulnerability, and accountability should be in the DNA of every fellowship. In addition, the following should be discussed:

1. Determine which of the following options are possible when mediating:
   a. Forgiveness and reconciliation and staying in the same fellowship.
   b. The offended parties forgive each other and amicably separate and go their own direction.
   c. The person(s) suffering from trauma needs trauma counselling.
2. Begin to write, collect, and share culturally appropriate, powerful, real stories on forgiveness, reconciliation, and restoration. This will give BMBs models that they can emulate.
3. Develop courses that deal with the complexities of the conflict in the North African, Middle Eastern, and Iranian contexts, that: a) exegete the scriptures, b) exegete the culture and context using global tools (see select bibliography below), and c) exegete the people and their complexities in conflict resolution.

The Role of the Global Church

The global church has wrestled with the complexities of mediation. Although the teaching may be more tailored to a particular context, like Western churches, the principles used can be applied to every culture when critical contextualisation is applied.

1. The Western church approaches mediation through definite, programmed, institutionalised relationships. Their approach through organisation can greatly help the nascent church to establish a structure to address strained relationships.
2. The global church can bring in teaching on the art of listening.
3. The global church has learned the art of mediation in the Truth and Reconciliation Commission in South Africa. These same principles can be applied in mediation in the Middle Eastern context.
4. The global church can provide mentors to help local mediators grow in wisdom and emotional maturity through seminars and walking alongside them doing mediation until they have gained the confidence and skills to be effective mediators.
5. The global church can help the BMB churches to identify what is mediation from a biblical perspective and how it should be intentional and how it should not be driven by the shame culture yet can be applied from the perspective of honour.

We are seeing God working in an unprecedented way in the Muslim world. Thousands are coming to Christ and churches are being planted. There is a focus on seeing churches established in areas that previously have seen little fruit. It is an exciting time in mission history. We live in a glocal world that is more interconnected than ever before. But there is a huge need for mature Christian BMB leaders to help the first-generation church grow and thrive in a hostile environment. We don't want to repeat what has happened in Bulgaria or Uyghurs in the 1990s who experienced rapid growth but, within the first generation, the believers stopped meeting together. The root cause was poor community formation and poor leadership. In this book, we have identified the problem areas, their complexities, and a pathway forward. The participants in this consultation discovered that we could discuss hard issues in a safe place. They found it liberating and encouraging. We pray that what is presented in this book will be repeated in many areas. We are not alone and the global church is ready to learn from our BMB brothers and sisters and stand ready to help so that we all "may be built up until we all reach unity in the faith and in the knowledge of the Son of God and become mature, attaining to the whole measure of the fullness of Christ" as is written in Ephesians 4:12-13.

Conclusion

We began by noting the dramatic change in Muslims coming to Christ worldwide and that these new disciples – referred to as BMBs – are facing challenges that need to be heard and not minimised. We see examples of these developments in parts of the MENA region. We seek to embrace these people within the global church of which all Christ's followers are members. Furthermore, this global community should be a place of mutual learning. This book, based on a consultation, is part of this rich dynamic.

Our specific focus here is on conflict, which we see as an inevitable consequence of the Fall. Rather than just managing conflict, we have set out to describe ways of resolving conflict by mediation, increased mutual understanding and a focus on biblical principles, especially concerning leadership.

For Iranian and Arab contexts, we have sought to explain the root causes of conflict within the cultural norms of these societies of which Christians are an integral component. This is the cultural heritage of newly emerging fellowships of Christ's followers. It is almost inevitable that new fellowships follow such norms for styles of leadership and conflict management.

As with all cultures, there are elements which need transforming to conform to Christ-like and biblical patterns of leadership and conflict management. For Arab and Iranian contexts, our intention here has been to show that the patterns commonly seen are not a surprise. Furthermore, we have sought to create a space for analysis, for deepening understanding and for seeking the Spirit's active assistance in bringing about transformation. We are aware that being counter-cultural is a necessary component of being Christ-like for us all, and that this is rarely comfortable or easy. It is, however, what Christ calls us to; it does express his kingdom; and at times, it is profoundly attractive to others.

We have noted that what we have at present is largely a first-generation church. Succeeding generations will be different.

We need to watch, pray, and guide as requested as God builds his church among Iranians and Arabs in the years ahead.

May the Lord God continue to build his church among Arab and Iranian peoples everywhere to the glory of the name of Jesus.

Abbreviations

BMB	believer from a Muslim background
BQ	biblical intelligence
DMM	discipleship making movements
EQ	emotional intelligence
IQ	intelligence
MBB	Muslim background believer
MENA	Middle East and North Africa
PBS	public broadcasting service
TTG	toward the goal

Glossary

al wasata	practice of mediation
shari'a	Islamic law; more broadly, the Muslim way of doing things
tov	Hebrew for good
ummah	worldwide Muslim community

References

Abu-Nimer, Mohammed. 1996. "Conflict Resolution Approaches: Western and Middle Eastern Lessons and Possibilities", *The American Journal of Economics and Sociology* 55(1): 35–52. [Available at: http://www.jstor.org/stable/3487672], [Last accessed: 28th September 2024].
Ainsworth, Mary D. Salter, Mary C. Blehar, Everett Waters, Sally N. Wall. 2015. *Patterns of Attachment: A Psychological Study of the Strange Situation.* London: Psychology Press & Routledge Classic Editions.
Arterburn, Stephen and Jack Felton. 2001. *Toxic Faith: Experiencing Healing from Painful Spiritual Abuse.* Colorado Springs, CO: Waterbrook Press.
——. 2000. *More Jesus, Less Religion: Moving from Rules to Relationship.* Colorado Springs, CO: Waterbrook Press.
Chinchen, Delbert. 1995. "The Patron-Client System: A Model of Indigenous Leadership", *Evangelical Missions Quarterly* 31(4): 446–451.
Cloud, Henry and John Townsend. 1996. *Boundaries: When to Say Yes, How to Say No.* Grand Rapids, MI: Zondervan.
——. 2016. *Safe People: How to Find Relationships that are Good for You and Avoid Those That Aren't.* Grand Rapids, MI: Zondervan.
Crabb, Larry. 2013. *Inside Out.* Colorado Springs, CO: NavPress.
Durie, Mark. 2010. *Liberty to the Captives: Freedom From Islam and Dhimmitude Through The Cross.* Melbourne, Australia: Deror Books.
Emmanuel, Mano. 2020. *Interpersonal Reconciliation Between Christians in a Shame-Oriented Culture.* Carlisle, UK: Langham Monographs.
Foster, Richard. 2009. *Money, Sex and Power: The Challenge of the Disciplined Life.* London: Hodder & Stoughton.
Garrison, David. 2014. *A Wind in the House of Islam: How God is Drawing Muslims Around the World to Faith in Jesus Christ.* Monument, CO: WIGTake Resources.
Green, Tim, and Roxy. 2016. *Joining the Family: The Book.* Birmingham, UK: Kitab-Interserve Resources.
Hibbert, Richard Y. 2013. "Why Do They Leave?: An Ethnographic Investigation of Defection from Turkish-Speaking Roma Churches in Bulgaria", *Missiology* 41(3): 315–328.
Hiebert, Paul G. 1987. "Critical Contextualization", *International Bulletin of Missionary Research* 11(3), (July 1987), 104–112. [Available at: https://journals.sagepub.com/doi/10.1177/239693938701100302], [Last accessed: 28th September 2024].
Hill, Harriet, Margaret Hill, Richard Bagge and Pat Miersma. 2014. *Healing the Wounds of Trauma: How the Church Can Help, Expanded Edition.* Trauma Healing Institute, American Bible Society.

Hofstede, Geert. 1991. *Cultures and Organizations: Software of the Mind.* London: McGraw-Hill.

———. 2001. *Cultures and Consequences: Comparing Values, Behaviors, Institutions and Organizations Across Nations.* 2nd ed. Thousand Oaks, CA: Sage.

House, R.J., P.J. Hanges, M. Javidan, P.W. Dorfman, and V. Gupta. 2004. *Culture, Leadership and Organizations: The GLOBE Study of 62 Societies.* Thousand Oaks, CA: Sage.

Irani, George E. 1999. "Islamic Mediation Techniques for Middle East Conflicts", In *Middle East Review of International Affairs* 3(2). [Available at: https://www.mediate.com/articles/mideast.cfm], [Last accessed: 28th September 2024].

Kehrein, Glen and Raleigh Washington. 1994. *Breaking Down Walls: A Model for Reconciliation in an Age of Racial Strife.* Chicago, IL: Moody Press.

Kuhn, Mike. 2009. *Fresh Vision for the Muslim World: An Incarnational Alternative.* Downers Grove, IL: IVP Books.

Lidstone, Julyan. 2019. *Give Up the Purple: A Call for Servant Leadership in Hierarchical Cultures.* Cumbria, UK: Langham Global Library.

Little, Don. 2015. *Effective Discipling in Muslim Communities: Scripture, History and Seasoned Practices.* Downers Grove, IL, IVP.

Manning, Brennan. 1997. *Abba's Child: The Cry of the Heart for Intimate Belonging.* Colorado Springs, CO: Navpress.

McGavran, Donald. 1974. *The Clash Between Christianity and Cultures.* Washington, DC: Canon Press.

McKnight, Scot, and Laura Barringer McKnight. 2020. *A Church Called Tov: Forming a Goodness Culture That Resists Abuses of Power and Promotes Healing.* Carol Stream, IL: Tyndale House.

Miller, Duane. 2016. *Living Among the Breakage: Contextual Theology-Making and Ex-Muslim Christians.* Eugene, OR: Pickwick Publications.

Muller, Roland. 2013. *The Messenger, The Message, and the Community: Three Critical Issues For the Cross-Cultural Church Planter.* Saskatchewan, Canada: CanBooks.

Nelson, Heather Davis. 2016. *Unashamed: Healing Our Brokenness and Finding Freedom From Shame.* Wheaton, IL: Crossway.

Niebuhr, H. Richard.1951. *Christ and Culture.* New York: Harper & Row.

Nouwen, Henri, J.M. 2002 [1989]. *In the Name of Jesus: Reflections on Christian Leadership.* Chestnut Ridge, NY: Crossroad.

Oksnevad, Roy. 2019. *The Burden of Baggage: First Generation Issues in Coming to Christ.* Littleton, CO: William Carey. Also in Farsi under the title: *Risen from Ashes to Christ: Understanding Muslim-Convert Churches through the Experience of Iranian Church*, [Available at: https://www.judeproject.org/online-store.html], [Last accessed: 28th September 2024].

Sande, Ken. 2004. *The Peace Maker: A Biblical Guide to Resolving Personal Conflict.* Grand Rapids, MI: Baker.

Scazzero, Peter. 2017. *Emotionally Healthy Spirituality: Discipleship that Deeply Changes Your Relationship with God.* Grand Rapids, MI: Zondervan. (For more information and further resources, see Emotionally Healthy website at: www.emotionallyhealthy.org, [Last accessed: 28th September 2024].
——. 2015. *The Emotionally Healthy Leader: How Transforming Your Inner Life Will Deeply Transform Your Church, Team, and the World.* Grand Rapids, MI: Zondervan.
——. 2003. *The Emotionally Healthy Church: A Strategy for Discipleship That Actually Changes Lives.* Grand Rapids, MI: Zondervan.
Schaeffer, Francis. 2006. *The Mark of the Christian.* Downers Grove, IL: IVP.
Shahverdyan, Rafi. 2018. *Armenian Wine, Turkish Bread: A Real-Life Journey of Reconciliation.* Pennsauken, NJ: BookBaby.
Stanley, Charles F. 2002. *The Gift of Forgiveness.* Nashville, TN: Thomas Nelson.
Volf, Miroslav. 2006. *Free of Charge: Giving and Forgiving in a Culture Stripped of Grace.* Grand Rapids, MI: Zondervan.
——. 1996. *Exclusion and Embrace: A Theological Exploration of Identity, Otherness, and Reconciliation.* Nashville, TN: Abingdon Press.
Walsh, Edward T. 2012. *Shame Interrupted: How God Lifts the Pain of Worthlessness and Rejection.* Greensboro, NC: New Growth Press.
Yancey, Phillip. 1995. *The Jesus I Never Knew.* Grand Rapids, MI: Zondervan.

Websites

Hofstede Insights: Consulting/Training/Certification/Tooling: "Country Comparison Tool", *The Culture Factor Group*, [Available at: https://www.theculturefactor.com/country-comparison-tool?countries=(], [Last accessed: 28th September 2024].

Resources for Trauma Healing

Trauma Healing Institute, "Free Resources", Webpage on Trauma Healing Institute's website. [Available at: https://traumahealinginstitute.org/free-downloads], [Last accessed: 28th September 2024].
American Group Psychotherapy Association, "What Every Person Should Know About Trauma", *AGPA Website*, [Available at: https://www.agpa.org/docs/default-source/practice-resources/what-every-person-should-know-about-trauma.pdf?sfvrsn=2], [Last accessed: 28th September 2024].

Made in the USA
Monee, IL
04 March 2025

13469574R00072